END THE STRUGGLE
and DANCE WITH LIFE

END THE STRUGGLE and DANCE WITH LIFE

HOW TO BUILD YOURSELF UP
WHEN THE WORLD GETS YOU DOWN

SUSAN JEFFERS, Ph.D.

ST. MARTIN'S PRESS
New York

Grateful acknowledgment is given for permission to reprint excerpts from the following: *The Magic of Conflict* by Thomas Crum. Copyright © 1987 by Thomas Crum. Reprinted by permission of Simon & Schuster, Inc.; *Zorba the Greek* by Nikos Kazantzakis. Copyright 1953 by Simon & Schuster, Inc. Copyright renewed © 1981 by Simon & Schuster, Inc. Reprinted by permission of Simon & Schuster, Inc.; *Burst Out Laughing* by Barry Stevens. Copyright © 1984 by Barry Stevens. Reprinted by permission of Celestial Arts, P.O. Box 7123, Berkeley, CA 94707; *Quantum Soup: Fortune Cookies in Crisis* by Chungliang Al Huang. Copyright © 1991 by Chungliang Al Huang. Reprinted by permission of Celestial Arts, P.O. Box 7123, Berkeley, CA 94707. Chapter Notes on pages 243–248 constitute a continuation of this copyright page.

Design by Michael Mendelsohn of MM Design 2000, Inc.

Library of Congress Cataloging-in-Publication Data

Jeffers, Susan J.
    End the struggle and dance with life : how to build yourself up when the world gets you down / by Susan Jeffers—1st ed.
        p. cm.
    Includes bibliographical references.
    ISBN 0-312-13967-5
    1. Peace of mind. 2. Contentment. 3. Joy. I. Title.
BF637.P3J44   1996
158'.1—dc20   95-25405
                                                                                 CIP

10 9 8 7 6 5 4 3 2

To my wonderful husband,

MARK SHELMERDINE,

with whom I want to dance for
the rest of my life!

CONTENTS

Contents

ACKNOWLEDGMENTS

The following people have eased my struggle and allowed me to dance with the writing of this book. I am forever grateful.

Dominick Abel, my literary agent who manages to guide me with great humor and sensitivity . . . and success! Thank you, Dominick.

Jennifer Enderlin, my editor at St. Martin's Press, whose enthusiasm and encouragement make my heart sing. Thank you, Jennifer.

Those in the field of "Spiritual" psychology, past and present, who have taught me a whole new dimension of being—body, mind, and Spirit. Thank you, dear teachers.

James Steen, W. Dean La Douceur, Edward Habib, and Anita Gershman, who all have made special contributions to this book. Thank you, James, Dean, Edward, and Anita.

The men and women whose stories add so much richness and authenticity to the content of this book. Thank you, beautiful people.

My readers, who have let me know that my writing has contributed to their lives. What a gift they have given me! Thank you, readers.

Leslie and Gerry Gershman, my children; Alice and Guy Shelmerdine, my stepchildren; and Meredith Marshall, my daughter-in-law. You all bring such energy, joy, and love into my life. Thank you, Leslie, Gerry, Alice, Guy, and Meredith.

Marcia Fleshel, my sister and dearest friend, with whom I laugh, dream, ponder, learn, and enjoy. And, of course, her husband, Jack, who brings us all so much love and laughter. Thank you, Marcia and Jack.

Mark Shelmerdine, my wonderful husband, who continues to pour countless riches into my life. Thank you, my dearest Mark.

do the work
let go of the fight
embrace the flow
bliss!

sj

END THE STRUGGLE
and DANCE WITH LIFE

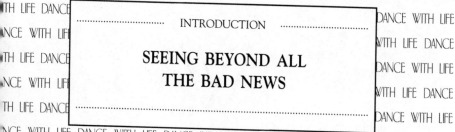

SEEING BEYOND ALL
THE BAD NEWS

E LIVE IN A DIFFICULT WORLD.
No doubt about it. And I am sure you have pondered the following questions, which seem to be on everyone's mind:

How can we enjoy our life in a world increasingly encased in struggle?

How do we stop the "efforting" and derive value and pleasure from all that we do?

How can we bring serenity into our everyday lives when we constantly feel as though we are hitting our heads against a wall?

How can we stop worrying when so many things seem to threaten us?

Challenging questions indeed! As I travel around the world in my role as author, workshop leader, and public speaker, I am struck by the battle with life that so many of us seem to be waging. Even in the absence of "war," *when things are going well*, the battle continues. We worry, obsess, and endlessly try to control everyone and everything around us. Not only do we try to control the present and the future, our minds futilely search for ways to re-create the past!

We yearn to feel calmer, more in control, and excited about life, but the possibility of that seems like a long-lost dream. The joy in living is gone. Our love of life is wearing thin. Something is very wrong. But what is it?

Observing what is happening in our world today, one might speculate that much of our unrest comes from a bad economy, rampant crime, terrible diseases, environmental disasters, and, on a more personal level, trouble in relationships, lack of money, job dissatisfaction, family responsibilities, and the like. It seems logical that all this bad news is at the root of our worry, anger, and frustration. Certainly it gives us something to blame!

And yet, are these potentially Soul-destroying circumstances the *real* cause of our constant struggle with life? They certainly offer us a great challenge, but we need to look a little deeper. I don't want to minimize the distress created by a home being destroyed in a hurricane, or illness in the family, or poverty, or the stress of earning a living. However, if you are a people watcher, as I am, you will notice a very intriguing difference in the way people react to potentially devastating situations. *Some react with despair and some with serenity.* What makes this puzzling difference?

After much research and personal experience, I have come to the conclusion that those who approach life with serenity rather than struggle have looked beyond the bad news and mastered the art of "dancing with life." And to me . . .

Dancing with life is moving into the flow of our experiences—*good or bad*—with a feeling of harmony, trust, gratitude, and love.

You may be thinking, I have trouble flowing with the good! How can I ever learn to flow with the bad? You've come to the right place!

I wrote *Feel the Fear and Do It Anyway* to help you feel more powerful in the face of your fears. Clearly, handling our fears is an essential part of the tapestry of a life well lived. *End the Struggle and Dance with Life* was written to help you with an equally important part of this great tapestry—easing the strain of everyday living and bringing into your life more enjoyment, appreciation, and peace. Those of you who are familiar with my work know that what I teach comes largely from my own Journey. This book is no exception. After pushing through much fear and creating a life that, on any objective level, was truly wonderful, I couldn't avoid noticing the intense feeling of struggle that I continued to experience. This sense of inner struggle was there *whether my external experiences were good or whether they were bad!* My search for the reasons why the struggle was there led me to many interesting insights about what makes life more difficult and what makes it easier. I offer this book as a way of sharing my new learning with you.

I suggest that you read through *End the Struggle and Dance with Life* once. Then go back to the beginning and incorporate—step-by-step—the concepts and exercises into your daily life. Always keep the book in a handy place. I have stacks of letters from people who have read *Feel the Fear and Do It Anyway*, telling me that when the old fear comes creeping in, they can open the book to any page and find the strength they need. So, too, with *End the Struggle and Dance with Life*. When life seems exhausting and difficult, you can open the book to any page and find the lightness and calm you need. Sometimes a gentle reminder of what life is *really* all about can make a world of difference.

I've come a long, long way on this issue of dancing with life, and I'm amazed at how obvious are the causes of our upsets in life, big and small. I'm reminded of the ancient saying,

"The road is smooth. Why do you throw rocks before you?"

We all throw rocks before us. One thing I've learned with certainty is that *it's very hard to dance on rocks.* So let's begin clearing the debris to make way for a more joyful, peaceful, and abundant life!

PART I

RISING ABOVE the CLOUDS

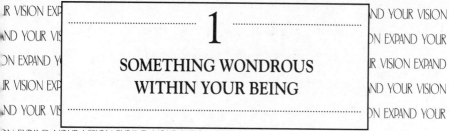

1

SOMETHING WONDROUS
WITHIN YOUR BEING

I prepared excitedly for my departure, as if this journey had a mysterious significance. I had decided to change my mode of life. "Till now," I told myself, "you have only seen the shadow and been well content with it; now, I am going to lead you to the substance."

Nikos Kazantzakis, Zorba the Greek[1]

....

I HAVE SITTING ON MY DESK A PINK quartz statue of a laughing Buddha. There is a look of ecstasy on his face as if he is basking in the warmth of the glorious sun. One might think he's ecstatic because he's a millionaire. But a millionaire he is not; in one hand he carries his begging bowl, and in the other he carries a sack, the container of all his belongings. One might think he's ecstatic because he's in great physical shape. But a Greek god he's certainly not; he has a huge belly and is definitely in need of a diet and a gym! One might think he's ecstatic because he's in a great relationship. But he travels alone. Then why *is* he so in love with life?

Legend has it that he is ecstatic because, contrary to most of us in today's world, he has discovered that the true joy in life does not come from mounds of money, a great body, a relationship, or anything else *out there*. He has discovered that the true joy in life comes from *something wondrous within his being*. He knows that this "something wondrous" is ever present and always accessible. As a result, he feels free, safe, complete, and truly able to dance with life.

Do we have to mimic the lifestyle of the laughing Buddha in order to feel joy and peace in life? Do we have to divest ourselves of our worldly belongings, put on weight, and travel alone in order to find the laughter? Hardly! What is required is that we, like the laughing Buddha, take the steps necessary to discover the something wondrous within our own being—the substance rather than the shadow—that allows us to become laughing lawyers, laughing sales clerks, laughing parents, laughing scientists, laughing factory workers, or laughing whatever we do in life.

What is that something wondrous within our being? And how do we bring it into our everyday lives so that we, too, can feel free, safe, complete, and truly able to dance with life? Perhaps we can find some clues from the humor of the following quote from some unknown sage:

> "Oriental man is very light up in the head and heavy down in the belly and feels very secure. Western man is light in the belly and very heavy up in the head, so he topples over."

As I interpret this little gem of wisdom, "Oriental man" refers to those whose upbringing has been filled with the Eastern teachings of Spirituality that balance us and bring us peace. "Western man" refers to those whose upbringing has been filled with the off-balance Western teachings of mind over spirit and struggle over peace. We topple over as our learned beliefs pull us away from the power and joy we hold inside—the something wondrous within our being.

I believe that there is a place within each and every one of us that is the source of all the Divine qualities such as love, caring, intuition, strength, appreciation, joy, bliss, and gratitude. When we "live" in that wondrous place, which I call the HIGHER SELF, we can't help but take into our being many of the qualities of the laughing Buddha. We are free to enjoy the best that life has to offer. Peace and laughter fill our hearts. We come out of the shadow and find the substance of a life well lived.

Many of us have great resistance to exploring the pathway that leads to the Higher Self, the Spiritual part of who we are. We resist for a variety of reasons:

Many wrongly associate Spirituality with organized religion when, in fact, organized religion sometimes pulls us away from the Spiritual part of who we are; for example, when it asks us to judge and exclude others for their different beliefs.

Many can't believe that they are more than they think they are. Therefore, they stay stuck in the negativity of the lowest part of their being.

Many simply can't understand that there could be other ways of seeing the world around them. They have an If-you-can't-see-it, it doesn't-exist kind of mentality.

All of this is very understandable. Our conditioning has brainwashed us into seeing the world from a very limited perspective. There is an old Yiddish saying,

"To a worm in horseradish, the whole world is horseradish."

Unfortunately, many of us are like those worms in horseradish! We see only through the eyes of our conditioning. We have been unwittingly *trained to worry, trained to struggle* by a society that thinks it is teaching us well but that doesn't understand the very fundamentals of a life well lived. And so we end up worrying and struggling. Many of us go to therapy. Although traditional psychotherapy may teach us to adjust to this world, it too often doesn't teach us how to rise above the clouds, to rise above the horseradish!

I remember the day my journey out of the horseradish and into a new life began. It seems like yesterday, although the year was 1972. I had just ended my marriage of many years and embarked on my first trip without my husband—a big step indeed! Fear dominated most of my being as I went through the motions of trying to enjoy myself in my chosen destination, Spain. I felt so far from home, so far from the safety, real or imagined, I had felt for so many years of married life. One morning I decided to visit the Alhambra, a beautiful national treasure in Spain. It was early morning and a slight chill was in the air. I stood alone in a magnificent garden looking at the scene before me. My sadness about my divorce couldn't dim the awesome sight of the beautiful city, distant mountains, and the sun's rays coming through the dispersing clouds.

I stood there for a few moments in deep appreciation of the riches before me, captivated by the stillness of the morning. And then something happened, something that took me out of the realm of ordinary experience and transported me into a new dimension of being. I suddenly felt myself being bathed in rays of glorious light as I melded into the magnificence surrounding me. On a deep cellular level, I became a part of it all. I was at one with the entire Universe. I felt a sense of exquisite safety, peace, and harmony—a sublime sense that all was well in my world, now and forever.

Yet the above does not even begin to portray the blissful state of being to which I was transported. The English language does not have the words to describe it. This state lasted only a few precious moments as other visitors to the garden broke my connection with the sublime and I was brought back into my commonplace way of seeing the world. But the experience was so profound that it changed my life forever.

For the very first time, I became aware that there was a dimension of my being (the substance instead of the shadow) that I had never known before, a transcendent part of who I was that was able to touch the divine energy of the entire Universe. It was a place of extraordinary peace, the kind of peace that was absent in my struggle-dominated world. All my personal problems relating to money, love, children, career, taxes, and the state of the world seemed like insignificant specks in a world that was so HUGELY more.

While I wasn't able to hold on to that transcendent state of being for more than a brief moment in time, I learned so much.

I learned that what I thought was the totality of my being was only an infinitesimally small part of a much larger whole.

I learned that there were dimensions of my being that I had never experienced or explored.

I learned that as much as I got caught in the melodrama of daily life, there was another way of seeing myself in this world.

In essence, I learned that there was much more than meets the eye . . . that is, once I could pull myself out of the horseradish!

With this astounding introduction to another way of being in this world, I knew it was time to stop, regroup, and begin a new Journey down a different pathway, the one that leads to a heaven on earth instead of a First-you-suffer, then-you-die kind of existence. This Journey has been the backbone of my life since that extraordinary day more than twenty years ago. It has led me to many wonderful (and challenging!) places inside and outside my being.

There are many others who have felt the life-altering power of such peak experiences, as I later learned they were called. Psychologist Abraham Maslow studied healthy people in the 1960s and discovered many who reported having such mystical experiences, moments of such intense rapture and awe that all fear and separation disappeared. They reported a sensation of becoming one with the Universe.

He noted that peak experiences don't happen to everyone, nor can they be willed into our lives. They seem to happen out of the blue. In fact, *if we try to make them happen, it's almost a guarantee that they won't!* He also noted that these peak experiences rarely had anything to do with religion. Some came from great moments of love and sex, from hearing beautiful music, from nature, from moments of awesome creativity, from meditation, from hobbies such as fishing, and even from moments of crisis. He found that even though they don't happen to everyone (*nor do they have to in order to have a wonderful life)*, they were far more common than he had expected.

It is only recently that Spiritual experiences of this kind are becoming part of normal, everyday conversations and consciousness. Up until now, people have been hesitant to talk about them, fearing they would be thought of as crazy. But we've reached a point where human beings in the mainstream *yearn* to know that the Spiritual part of who they are really exists. The word "Spirit" is now on the lips of bank managers, teachers, soldiers, prisoners, housewives, attorneys, and all segments of our society. This is great news! It means that as a society we are climbing out of the mire of our horseradish into a more beautiful world.

Thankfully, we as individuals don't have to wait for society as a whole to change. Nor do we have to wait for a peak experience to propel us into the world of the Spirit. We can begin the Journey toward that something wondrous within our being right now, right where we are, and with the tools that are presently in our grasp. All we need is an awareness that there is more to life than the petty pace at which most of us live our lives today. (You can't get out of the horseradish unless you know you're in it!) Once that awareness is there, the Journey inward to the Higher Self can begin, and life can expand to encompass a world that is HUGE with possibility.

To offer you a strong inducement to make that Journey an integral part of your life, let me make it clear that . . .

Bringing a Spiritual dimension into all that we do is essential for ending the struggle and dancing with life. Our body and our minds can take us only so far. Our Spirit can lead us all the way Home.

I believe that it is *always* our Spiritual separation that causes our intense sense of struggle, in good times and in bad. Without touching the Spiritual part of who we are, peace is absent, or at best fleeting.

Because our society focuses on externals, we have not been taught how to bring the Spirit into our everyday life. In fact, we've been taught very little about the Spirit at all. But that needn't stop us from learning about it ourselves. I remember taking off in an airplane on a very cloudy day. The plane climbed and climbed through the fog and dense cloud cover. It was very dark and gloomy and, to some, very frightening. At one point, the clouds began to lighten and, all of a sudden, the plane burst through into the glorious light of the sun. It was hard to believe that reaching a place of intense clarity and light was simply a matter of rising above the clouds.

It occurred to me that my experience in the plane was a great metaphor for how many of us live our lives. Most of the time, we are immersed in fog and heaviness, not understanding that all we have to do is learn how to fly above the clouds. And that's what transcending to the level of the Higher Self allows us to do—transcend the petty and focus on what is truly wonderful about living.

There are many ways to get in touch with the Higher Self, the Spiritual part of who we are. One of the most delightful stories demonstrating this fact comes from Ram Dass.[2] In the early 1970s he was addressing a room full of flower children, many of whom had found their Spiritual awakening through the use of psychedelic drugs. As he describes it, most of them were wearing white with flowers around their necks, and they were smiling a lot. Ram Dass certainly fit into the scene with his long beard and beads.

As he looked out into his audience, his vision was drawn to an elderly woman sitting in the front row. Her oxford shoes, little hat with fake cherries, and black patent-leather bag didn't fit the picture. As he talked, he noticed her nodding with an obvious sense of agreement to what he was saying. The more far out and outrageous his lecture became, the more she nodded.

When the lecture was over, she came up and thanked him profusely for his wisdom and let him know that everything he talked about was also her experience of the Universe. In great confusion, he asked, "How do you *know?* What have you done that has given you these kinds of out-of-this-world experiences." She leaned forward and whispered to him conspiratorially, "I crochet."

It was then that he understood that there are many ways to the same destination. Her pathway into a Spiritual or transcendent state was crocheting. I'll wager that crocheting is not your pathway into the Spiritual part of who you are (nor are psychedelic drugs!), but there are many simple and joyous life-transforming ways to the Higher Self, many of which are revealed in this book. No matter where you are in your life's Journey, there is always so much more to explore within your being. Ours is a lifelong opportunity to discover more and more about that something wondrous within our being.

When I was a little girl, my father used to tell me that "life is a mass of boredom, interjected with a few exquisite moments." Poor Dad! He didn't know life could be any other way. And for many years I believed him. But not anymore. I wish he were still alive so that I could tell him that he was mistaken, that in fact, even with the tears that are a normal part of living, *life can be a mass of exquisite moments interjected with a few moments of boredom.* And I would lovingly show him how to put more exquisite moments in his life. Well, he isn't alive today. But *you* are! And I've designed each of the following chapters to introduce more and more moments of exquisiteness into your life.

The next section (Part II) shows you how to RELEASE—to let go of the many actions and beliefs that keep you drowning in struggle. The last section (Part III) shows you how to EMBRACE—to take in the incredible beauty and richness in your life that up until now has gone virtually unnoticed. When you learn the art of releasing the darkness and embracing the light, you will have learned all you ever need to know about ending the struggle and dancing with life.

When this happens, you notice a very strange phenomenon: Each time you look into the mirror, you are able to see the ecstatic face of the laughing Buddha reflected in your eyes. You will have discovered that something wondrous within your being, which, when all is said and done, is the only thing that any of us has ever been searching for!

It won't happen overnight, but with each little step, you will find life getting better and better and better and better. A Tibetan lama once crossed the Himalayas on foot during the Chinese occupation of his country. When asked how he had managed such a difficult journey, he answered, "That's simple. One step at a time." That's all it takes—one step at a time. Be good to yourself. *Begin the Journey now.*

PART II

RELEASING

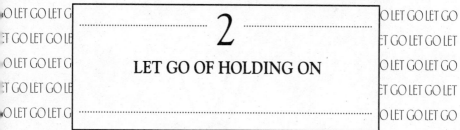

2

LET GO OF HOLDING ON

WHAT A LOVELY IMAGE—WEARING this world just as a loose garment. What came to me when I first saw this quotation were the words . . .

FREE
EASY
COMFORTABLE
SOFT
FLEXIBLE
FLOWING
DANCING

Yes, that's the way we *all* want to wear life. Most of us, however, wear it like a girdle—tight, hard, rigid, uncomfortable, and constricting. Oh, how we long to take off that girdle and breathe deeply and freely! Oh, how we long to let go of all those things that keep us immersed in struggle instead of flying above the clouds!

Wearing the world as a loose garment means . . .

—letting go and cutting the cord that keeps us a prisoner,

—not hanging on so tightly to the way it's "supposed" to be,

—trusting that all is well, that life is happening perfectly,

–seeing the possibility of love and growth that exists in all experiences, good or bad,

–recognizing that the ebb and flow of life can be faced from a place of harmony instead of struggle.

What stops us from wearing the world as a loose garment? What keeps us bound up and rigid? When we look for an answer to these questions, our tendency is to look around and blame everything on what is "wrong" in our lives and in our world. And usually we can find much to blame. "If only this wasn't happening." "If only that was different."

Thankfully, our consciousness is beginning to change. More and more books are being written (and read!) that suggest that our inability to let go and enjoy life has nothing to do with anything *out there*. It has to do with what is going on *inside*. We are awakening to the fact that when things are not all right in our external world, something is not all right within our being.

As we take a look inside, we notice that something about our inability to let go suggests an *addiction to control*. Noted author and workshop leader Ken Keyes Jr. describes the symptoms of an addiction:

1. It creates tension in your body;
2. It makes you experience separating emotions such as resentment, anger, and fear instead of unifying emotions which give you experiences of acceptance, love, and joy;
3. Your mind tells you things must be different in order for you to enjoy life here and now;
4. Your mind makes you think there is something important to win or lose in this situation;
5. You feel that you have a "problem" in your life—instead of experiencing life as an enjoyable "game" to be played.[1]

Does all this sound too familiar? Is it possible you are addicted to control—like the rest of us?

The good news is that addictions can be overcome. *We don't have to live a life controlled by our need to control!* We can learn how to let go, thus feeling more comfortable, soft, flexible, and flowing about life—like wearing the world just as a loose garment.

How do we begin? I believe that *all* addictions are a function of the LOWER SELF. Let me introduce you to the Lower Self:

The Lower Self is the part of us that has been very badly educated to think that the only way to survive is to be numb to the feelings of others.

The Lower Self is the part of us that absorbs the teachings of our society and, as a result, is caught in the treadmill of more-better-best.

The Lower Self has heard all the admonitions and believes that the world is out to get us.

The Lower Self acts as a frightened parent who does not trust in our ability to handle all the threats in our life.

The Lower Self has no vision and does not understand that all situations in our life, good and bad, can be used as a teaching for our highest good.

Because of all of the above, anytime there is any sign of a real or imagined external threat, the Lower Self automatically triggers our need to control.

The way we can handle our addiction to control, therefore, is to pull ourselves away from the fear tactics of our Lower Self and rise to the level of our Higher Self, the Spiritual part of who we are, where we find true safety. We learn that:

The Higher Self is the dwelling place of all good things such as love, power, creativity, joy, satisfaction, and abundance.

The Higher Self knows we have the strength to handle anything that can ever happen to us.

The Higher Self doesn't see the outside world as a threat to our lives; it sees it as a place to learn and grow and contribute.

The Higher Self has great vision and can guide us to where we need to go with our lives.

The Higher Self knows that all situations in our life, good or bad, can be used as a teaching for our highest good.

Because of all of the above, anytime there is a sign of a real or imagined external threat, the Higher Self calms us down and assures us that all is well. As a result, we feel no need to shore up, defend, build walls, and hang on to those imagined pockets of safety. There is no need to control everything and everyone around us. In the realm of the Higher Self, we can say to ourselves:

It's all happening perfectly. Whatever happens in my life, I'll handle it. I'll learn from it. I'll make it a triumph!

For the skeptics out there, I know the concept of the Higher Self and Lower Self may be hard to accept. If you are one of them, I ask you to scan the events of your own life. As you do, you will realize that there were moments when everything was a struggle and fear dominated your emotions. There were other moments when everything seemed to flow and you were at peace. I am simply identifying the former moments as Lower-Self moments and the latter as Higher-Self moments.*

Given this differentiation, I'm sure you will agree that the key to ending the struggle and dancing with life is to create as many Higher-Self moments in your life as you can, despite what is happening in your external world. The tools I am providing can help

---

*If you can't find any of these Higher-Self moments as you scan the events of your life, NOT TO WORRY! As you regularly use the tools provided here, such moments will begin to appear.

you make that leap upward. And you will notice how freeing it is to leave your Lower Self behind!

The irony inherent in our attempts to control everyone and everything around us is the fact that *very little in the world is controllable*. Even when we *think* we are controlling something or someone out there, our efforts are misplaced. In truth,

The only thing we can effectively control is our *reactions* to whatever life hands us.

And in the final analysis, what can be more powerful than that! When we are in control of our reactions, we can be battered by the world around us and still maintain an inner sense of peace.

I love the story of the monk who was confronted by an angry warrior who said, "Don't you know who I am? I am someone who can cut off your head and not bat an eye!" The little monk looked him in the eyes and calmly replied, "Don't you know who I am? I am someone who can have you cut off my head . . . and not bat an eye!" Now that's the ultimate in controlling our reactions to whatever life hands us, the ultimate in wearing the world as a loose garment!

Most of us don't attain the ultimate enlightenment of our fearless monk, but we can still learn many of the principles of inner peace that he demonstrated. We can begin to let go of our addictive demands and flow with the events in our life over which we have little or no control.

You can see how learning the art of letting go is essential to our ending the struggle and dancing with life. We can't become laughing Buddhas by being compulsive, obsessive, fearful, and untrusting. The prison of the Lower Self keeps us from exploring paths that lead to self-fulfillment. Even though we think we are giving ourselves protection by seeking to control everything out there, we now know this is simply an illusion.

So let's look at a number of areas in our lives and see how we can release our addiction to control by rising above the addictive demands of the Lower Self to the truly powerful level of the Higher Self. As you read, think carefully about your own life and begin to see how you can personalize the suggestions I make. You will note that as you apply the letting go process to all the difficult areas of your life, you will automatically feel lighter and breathe easier.

Remember,

> **If you have external freedom but never rise above the level of the Lower Self, you will never feel free. If you have internal freedom and are able to rise above the level of the Lower Self, you will always feel free—*despite what is happening externally!***

Your inner peace has nothing to do with the dramas of your life. (What a relief!) When you find your way to your Higher Self, the Buddha inside of you will truly begin to laugh!

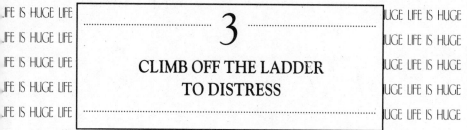

3

CLIMB OFF THE LADDER
TO DISTRESS

THAT'S A THOUGHT TO SEND SHIV-ers down your spine. Spending your whole life climbing a ladder only to discover it's against the wrong wall! Could this wise person be describing what is happening to so many of us today? I'm afraid so! Think about it:

If we had our ladder resting on the *right* wall, with every step we took we would feel more joyous, more fulfilled, happier, lighter, and all good things.

Yes, we would be on our way to ending the struggle and danc-ing with life! But look around. Evidence of struggle, fear, pain, frustration, and emptiness is everywhere. With every step we take, too many of us find ourselves overworked, hassled, and pulled in every direction with little payoff. Our children are lost and con-fused. Relationships are messed up. We live with a gnawing sense of scarcity, despite how much we accumulate. Some of us drop out, tired and angry that the climb is just too much.

So what terrible wall do we have our ladder resting on that is causing such distress? That wall, of course, is the wall leading to SUCCESS. At a very young age, we were trained by all those who had our best interests at heart to CLIMB THE LADDER TO SUCCESS. After all, isn't that the so-called American dream?* Isn't it almost patriotic to climb the ladder to success? You bet it is! And so, like all good little boys and girls, we began our climb. And we've been climbing ever since. But, sadly, we derive very little satisfaction and joy as a result of all of our efforts. Perhaps the American dream has become the American nightmare! Let's look at it.

How many of you got married and had children and thought you would be happy? *But you were not happy?* How many of you got the education you wanted and thought you would be happy? *But you were not happy?* How many of you got the job you wanted, the money you wanted, the man or woman you wanted, the weight you wanted, the divorce you wanted, and thought you would be happy? *But you were not happy?*

How many times did you earn some dreamed of goal only to re-alize *you needed more?* And then you earned more and realized it wasn't enough. You needed more. Then you earned still more and it wasn't enough. *You needed more and more and more and more.*

The truth is that we could climb and climb that ladder to suc-cess forever and *never* find the joy and satisfaction we are all seeking. Even those who make it all the way to the top are struck by the poignancy of Alfie's now-famous question:

"Decent clothes . . . a car . . . but what's it all about?"[1]

What IS it all about? It's becoming clear that it's not about what we thought it was about! It's becoming clear that the ladder to success has become the ladder to distress! So where do we go from here?

I believe that the root of the problem has to do with our present-day *definition* of SUCCESS. Webster's dictionary defines it as "the attainment of wealth, position, honors or the like."[2] It sounds worthy, even noble. But there are three essential flaws in this definition.

---

*A version of the American dream exists in all countries where success is determined by ex-ternal gain.

1. **The focus is only on the end product.** It is totally goal oriented. Nothing is said about the quality of our life as we make that climb up the ladder. Is it success when we give up a balanced and full life to pursue our wealth, position, honors, and the like? Or mess up our relationships? Or have a lousy time along the way? Not in my book. *Making it is painful in the context of an empty life.*

2. **The focus is on competition instead of partnership.** Competition, as a way of life, creates a feeling of alienation from others. As a result, we feel the truth of what we have always been told: We live in a dog-eat-dog world. Living in a dog-eat-dog world does not create a feeling of peace! *Making it is painful when we wake up each morning facing another battle to fight.*

3. **The focus is almost exclusively on external gain.** Our present-day ladder to success ignores the attainment of inner riches—peace, joy, caring, love, appreciation, and gratitude—all of which are necessary for ending the struggle and dancing with life. *Making it is painful when we are Spiritually bankrupt and unable to enjoy any of our rewards.*

The reason for all this bad news is that the basic tenets of success as we know it today are firmly situated in the seat of the Lower Self. Because the Lower Self is fear-based, it seeks control at all costs. When we operate from the level of the Lower Self, we cannot see the bigger picture. We cannot see the sun shining above the clouds. Fear makes us operate at the basest level of our being. *When we look at the way many of us behave as we climb the ladder to success, it is not a pretty picture!* And we wonder why we have an epidemic of low self-esteem in our society!

Obviously, there are some disturbing oversights inherent in the teachings of Western society when it comes to the concept of success. These oversights have created a great deal of misery within our being and in our world. Author Walter Cooper has some strong words to say about the matter:

"At no time in the history of humankind have so many souls been spiritually so betrayed by the cultural pollution in which they live."[3]

Perhaps he's justified in his sharp criticism. Think about it. Our society is structured in a way that almost guarantees our struggling with life. From the minute we are born we go into what Spiritual teacher Ram Dass calls "Somebody Training."[4] In order to be a "Somebody," we have to *pull into our lives* money, power, status, looks, prizes, awards, and any other external form of identity that will convince us—and others—that we are "enough." As we struggle to *pull in* all the goodies, we are *pulled out* of our center of power and love. And we find ourselves on the endless treadmill of . . .

> more-better-best . . .
> more-better-best . . .
> more-better-best . . .
> more-better-best . . .
> more-better-best . . .
> more-better-best . . .

Talk about struggle! At an early age, we become addicted to the process. Each success in the framework of more-better-best is like a fix. But fixes don't last very long, and we begin to crave more. Because we are stuck in the arena of the Lower Self rather than the Higher Self, we never feel we *have* enough, nor do we feel we ever *are* enough.

I'm sure you'll agree that walking the treadmill of more-better-best is a guaranteed way to keep us in a state of physical, psychic, and mental exhaustion. And sadly,

As we climb our ladder to success, instead of feeling like a Somebody, we end up feeling like a Nobody! We totally lose sight of that "something wondrous within our being." THAT, IN A NUTSHELL, IS THE FAILURE OF SUCCESS AS WE KNOW IT TODAY.

On some level, we know that something is terribly wrong with this model. Yet our addiction makes us hold on for dear life. No matter how much unhappiness our present-day definition of success brings us, we keep following societies rules of more-better-best; we continue to believe that competition is the only way to go; we keep looking outside for all of our joy and satisfaction. And we never find the proverbial cheese at the end of the tunnel. Yet we keep going down the same tunnel over and over and over again, not exploring other possibilities. I'm here to suggest that . . .

MAYBE THERE'S A BETTER WAY!

The fact that you are reading this book suggests that you are already asking yourself the very important question, "Is this all there is?" This means that you are ready to climb out of the horseradish of your conditioning and open up to the possibility of another way; you are ready to expand the dimensions of your being to encompass what is really grand about life and living; you are ready to move your ladder to another wall!

So how do we even begin to let go of our destructive addiction to more-better-best and embrace happier and more productive alternatives? I suggest that we begin by investigating a new definition of SUCCESS. It could look something like this:

SUCCESS is living a full and balanced life in partnership with others to create a joyful feeling of love, contribution, appreciation, and abundance, despite how our endeavors may turn out.

(I wonder if Webster's Dictionary would include this in their next edition!) This simple definition is filled with Higher-Self gifts that can transform a life of struggle into a life of joy. When we climb the ladder to such a Spiritually oriented definition of success, life takes on new meaning: We begin to focus on the process instead of the outcome; we begin to move away from the alienation of competition and immerse ourselves in the rewards of partnership; and we begin to gather inner values that reflect the huge amount of power and love we hold inside. By definition, we have our ladder resting on the right wall!

The rest of the chapter explores each of these Higher-Self gifts.

You will see that with this new definition of success, making it takes on a totally different meaning.

FOCUS ON THE PROCESS INSTEAD OF THE OUTCOME

LIFE IS HUGE! LIFE IS TO BE ENJOYED! When we are totally focused on the attainment of goals we have set for ourselves, we miss the expansiveness and richness of life NOW. We are constantly waiting for *the big moment* when our goals, dreams, desires, and aspirations will be fulfilled. That *guarantees* us a life that feels like a mass of boredom interjected with a few exquisite moments. What a waste of a life!

Understand that I'm not suggesting that goals, dreams, desires, and aspirations be eliminated. They add a certain richness to life. Yet we are foolish to depend on them for our happiness. Why put off living a rich life until our goals are reached? Why not embrace the totality of life NOW? Why wait another moment? And then, if we delightfully achieve some of our goals, it's pure gravy, not the substance of our life. And just as important, even if we don't achieve some of our goals, we haven't missed a thing. We've had a wonderful time along the way!

The latter chapters of this book have many exquisite pathways for helping you to learn the art of embracing life NOW, but let me begin to set the stage. First, you can begin the process of focusing on the NOW by creating a life that is so HUGE that the absence or loss of any one part of it doesn't wipe you out. Obviously when we have such a rich life, the outcomes of our endeavors lose some of their importance. That's a relief!

What does a HUGE life look like? It is a life that is filled with many *equally important* components. These include career, family, friends, hobbies, personal growth, contribution to the community, relationships, alone time, and whatever else rounds out a full life for you. Many of us have these components in our lives, but we often neglect them as we work to attain goals we have set up for ourselves. Hence, the key words in my definition of a huge life are "equally important."

When we are focused only on attaining future goals, we by definition live with a poverty mentality. When we live in the NOW, giving equal importance to ALL areas of our life, then life becomes HUGE and we feel the abundance!

Giving equal importance, of course, implies that we are committing 100 percent to all aspects of our life by giving them the attention and care they deserve; that is, we are equalizing our priorities knowing that IT'S *ALL* IMPORTANT! When we do this, we begin to enter the realm of the Higher Self and a wonderful transformation begins to happen.

We become bigger than we thought we were as we learn that we are *more than* our goals, our outcomes, our honors, and so on.

We aren't wiped out if something doesn't turn out the way we wanted it to.

We begin to acknowledge the incredible richness of our life.

We realize there is so much for which to be grateful.

Most important, *we realize that our goals are part of playing with life, but they are not our life*.

Living then becomes a moment-by-moment noticing of the enormity of our circle of being. Because we have equalized our priorities, we are feeling fulfilled whether we are . . .

spending an hour talking to a child or making a grand decision as the head of a large corporation or filling our garden with beautiful flowers or writing a book or washing the dishes or volunteering to help raise money for a cause or helping a friend get through a difficult time or reading a book or sitting and watching the sunset or building a roaring fire or preparing a delicious meal or—WHATEVER!

In this context, so-called ordinary everyday experiences become exquisite moments. They are the substance of life. In contrast, goals are not about substance, they are about shadow. They are possible happenings in the future and have nothing to do with NOW. If we fill our lives only with distant goals, our lives, by definition, feel empty NOW. Again, goals are important and fun to play with, but . . .

GOALS ARE NOT OUR LIFE! NOW IS OUR LIFE!

When we equalize our priorities, we are on the right track. We realize that all aspects of our life are important and worth enjoying. We realize they are all deserving of our commitment and caring. We realize that . . .

We are not simply machines trying to reach a destination. We are hearts and souls vibrantly connected to everyone and everything around us each moment of every day!

What I have been talking about is bringing more of the Spirit into everyday life. Contrary to popular opinion, to be Spiritual is not to get *out of* the world, but to be more fully *in it*—connected, joyful, and abundant.

I know this equalizing our priorities isn't easy to do. In fact, in the beginning, it seems like a contradiction in terms. Yet it is the key to breaking the chains of a powerful addiction to future outcomes.

Paradoxically, you may be surprised to find that as you let go of the obsessiveness that the goal-oriented mentality creates, many more of your goals will be reached easily and effortlessly. There is something incredibly magnetic about people who thoroughly enjoy their lives, who are relaxed about the outcome of all their endeavors, and who have an aura of expansion and appreciation. These people automatically seem to draw to themselves the better things in life.

Again, awareness is the key. Put a sign everywhere you can see it that simply says . . .

IT'S ALL IMPORTANT!

In this way, you will find that any of the boredom of your life will immediately be replaced by a mass of exquisite moments. And amassing exquisite moments is what it is all about!

MOVE AWAY FROM THE ALIENATION OF COMPETITION .

The more-better-best syndrome by definition sets up an atmosphere of exhausting and Soul-destroying competition. We can begin letting go of this need to outrun and outdo and outclass and outshine everyone else by incorporating into our everyday vocabulary a very important word:

ENOUGH!

ENOUGH is the amazing word that diminishes the power of more-better-best. It implies a sense of fullness and okayness. When we say, "I've had enough" at the end of a delicious meal, it means we are full and satisfied. We are not looking for more-better-best. The word ENOUGH has power behind it. When we include thoughts of ENOUGH in the deepest recesses of our being, we can begin to relax and smell the proverbial roses. Let me give you an example of how that works.

A while ago, I gave a talk at an all-day symposium. Three other speakers were on the schedule, all of whom were household names in the self-help field. As I was getting ready to walk on the stage to face three-thousand people sitting in the audience, my adrenaline was flowing big time! My husband, Mark, kissed me on the cheek and whispered in my ear, "You'll be the best."

In the past, I had loved hearing that, I *needed* to hear that! But this time, something didn't feel right about it. I suddenly became aware of the negative consequences of trying to be "the best." It created tension; it created alienation from the other speakers; and it took me off my Higher-Self purpose, which was to help others. As this Aha! hit me, I whispered in Mark's ear, "Thanks for the loving support, but next time just say, 'You'll be good enough.'" And with that letting go of my need to be the best, I walked confidently onto the stage, knowing that my only purpose was to put love into this world, *not to compete with other people who are trying to put their love into the world as well.*

It has been vehemently argued that competition is necessary in order for us to become better performers. I, and others, question this assumption.[5] In this particular case, feeling relieved of the burden of having to be the best, I connected with my audience better than I ever had before. I flowed. I was at ease. I was there simply to give what I had to give . . . out of love, not out of fear of not being the best. *Without the need to compete, I gave the best talk I had ever given.* So much for competition being necessary to improve performance!

Even with this awareness, you will notice that the overwhelming desire to be the best will constantly come up for you as you move from situation to situation in your life. Our conditioning is very strong. It is necessary for us to unlearn years of training in order to get off the treadmill of more-better-best. But as you let go of needing to be the best, you will find that *instead of your performance being diminished, it will soar as the fear, greed, and scarcity melt away.*

Understand that it's not that excellence can't result from competition. It certainly can. But competition as we know it today is crazy making and demoralizing. Why drive yourself crazy and live in a state of Spiritual deprivation when there is an alternative? Excellence *also* results from the simple knowing that you have a higher meaning and purpose in this world in whatever form that takes. This knowing brings us peace and confidence. And as icing on the cake,

> **When we have that sense of higher meaning and purpose, our "performance" is without equal.**

The belief that we need to compete in order to expand our ability is part of the Spiritual betrayal of the Lower Self. As we rid ourselves of the need to compete, we are truly free to move beyond our self-imposed limitations.

You may be wondering, "Can this idea possibly work in an arena that is as highly dependent on competition as sports?" I believe it can. Certainly, our focus on winning as the only goal has soured the entire athletic arena to a deadly degree. We need only notice the violence and malevolence all the way from our children's schoolyards to the once noble Olympic events. Terrible injuries, violence, anger, self-flagellation, and even death are common. Yet I have heard so many claim that the athletic field is a training ground for cooperation. While there may be pockets of playing fields where this is true, generally speaking it is not true. In fact, the title of a 1994 CNN television show about sports, *Field of Screams*, is very revealing.

I was very moved by a copy of a letter I received from James W. Steen, a Canadian coach and former international-level athlete. The letter was part of his ongoing efforts to counter the damage being done to children and carried into adulthood as a result of the present-day obsession by their elders to WIN at all costs. Written to the Canadian federal minister responsible for amateur sports, it was about the need to restore the only values that he felt could justify the public funding for athletics. He wrote:

> "We see eight-to-ten-year-old children being screamed at while struggling against hills designed to break the backs of Olympians: 'GO Joey!' 'PUSH Joey!' 'WIN Joey!' 'You have to want it, Joey!' The little Joey's don't want it, but scramble valiantly on without any technique or skill to offset the ebbing strength of their immature bodies. The shame of failure seems the only driving force. We have seen the highest levels of officialdom witness such nonsense, or more to the point—abuse—without taking the slightest notice. Their concerns are obviously in a different sphere. The mania to win can only translate into losing on all fronts."

Remember, these are words coming from a superior athlete with a true love for sports who still competes and coaches at levels rang-

ing from children to high-performance athletes at World Cups! He
goes on to say:

> "Sports, more than anything, is a way for youngsters to learn
> that their competitor on the 'field of honour' is not their ad-
> versary, but their partner and to learn that the object is not
> to beat her or him, but to bring out the best in both and grow
> together with generosity, honesty, loyalty, and respect."[6]

As it stands, the arena of athletics has become a sad mass of destructive and violent behavior that comes from the Lower Self. Here,
honor is long forgotten. I'm sure you can cite instances where this is
not the case, but in the larger picture, the field of athletics has lost
touch with the Higher-Self ideals of entering the arena in a spirit of
mutual growth. It would be wonderful if we could transform the playing field into its potentially life-enhancing magnificence.

Perhaps athletics is simply mirroring what is happening in the rest
of our world. In government, in business, in education, and within
families the goal of winning *at any cost* (including cheating and violence, if that is what it takes) is paramount, and as a result NOBODY
WINS. Everyone loses on all fronts. We pay with intense feelings of
struggle and, ultimately, diminished self-esteem. We miss the point
of living and loving as we focus only on the goal of winning.

It seems essential to me that we learn how to transform the field
of win-or-lose into a field of honor in all our endeavors. While we
can't change the world (at least not immediately!), we can begin
the process of pulling ourselves out of the quagmire of the negativity
of competition as it exists today. When we see our "opponents" as
allies, whether on the field of athletics or in business or wherever,
the world takes on a different energy. With a friendly challenge from
a talented "partner," we become more focused on expanding our
skills. We align ourselves—body, mind, and Spirit—to bring forth
the best that we have to offer. When this happens, we truly do become allies helping each other improve our skills, and the whole energy of the game of life is altered. Here, there need not be any loser.
In this game, both can win.

I have heard tennis players saying they love to play with really good opponents. Win or lose, their game improves. Their opponents have become their allies. In this kind of arena, we know we are enough. We play the game of life not with obsession but with a loving heart and a desire to expand to the best of our ability. To me, this is what the field of honor is all about.

Joy comes from expanding our abilities. We are not meant to be apathetic. We are meant to be used. We are meant to fill the world with caring and excellence in whatever field we choose. When we go for the proverbial jugular, however, it's our clue that we really don't feel we are enough. At such times, we need to keep reminding ourselves . . .

I AM ENOUGH.
I AM ENOUGH.
I AM ENOUGH.
I AM ENOUGH.
I AM ENOUGH.

By simply learning how to incorporate ENOUGH into our vocabulary, we have come a long way toward taking some pressure off of ourselves, and our struggle immediately begins to diminish.

FOCUS ON INTERNAL JOY AND SATISFACTION

The dictionary definition of success says nothing about love, joy, contribution, appreciation, and abundance—all internal measures of a life well lived. So as we go about cultivating the externals of our lives, we do nothing to cultivate the internals. Again, it's not that external success is bad; it's simply that when we focus *only* outward, we lose the essence of a life well lived and we push away one of our greatest pillars of strength—our Spiritual magnificence.

In our society, we are not trained to use the power of the Spiritual part of who we are—and it is a great power indeed. This is the hidden strength that emerges to lift a car if a loved one is trapped underneath; this is the hidden strength that emerges when we face really difficult times and come out enriched. This Spiritual part of who we are holds wisdom beyond our wildest dreams that can lead us to exactly where we need to go for our highest good—if we listen.

Because we are not trained to use the power that lies within, we feel weak and overwhelmed much of the time.

If we could train that muscle to the Higher Self, we would find our strength returning, and life wouldn't seem like such a struggle.

In addition, we wouldn't be so addicted to external gratification. If something didn't go right in the world out there, we wouldn't be tossed around like a puppet on a string. We would have a place of peace to which we could return over and over again, a place that gives us the needed assurance that on a Higher plane,

IT'S ALL HAPPENING PERFECTLY.

This place of peace is always there despite what is happening in the outside world. It is there when our business isn't doing well; it is there when our children are ill; it is there when we have bills to pay; it is there through all the difficulties (and joys) that life has to offer. When we come from a deep knowing that the place of peace is always there and we have learned how to find it, then by definition our feeling of struggle is greatly diminished.

Hence, climbing the ladder to our new definition of SUCCESS definitely includes learning how to embrace the power and love we hold inside. In this way, we need not depend on anything that is happening in the outside world. We have found our anchor in a stormy sea.

Bo Lozoff reminds us that everything out there is a "prop."[7] I like that analogy. When we seek only props, we feel empty. When we seek the inner substance, we begin to feel happily satisfied. The good news is that we can use all our experiences—good or bad—to teach us how to find the inner substance. In fact, sometimes our most difficult experiences speed the process. In truly difficult times, where else is there to go but inside? Using our worst times as tools for Spiritual expansion takes us out of the realm of victim (a horribly powerless place to be!) and puts us in the realm of creator of our own experience of life. That's powerful!

Let me end this chapter with a poignant metaphor. It is said that monkey hunters in India have a foolproof way of capturing monkeys. They hollow out a hole in a coconut and put candies inside. The hole is large enough for a monkey to squeeze his empty hand into, but not large enough to pull out a fistful of candies. The coconut is then staked into the ground.

It's only a matter of time before a monkey comes along and discovers the coconut. He reaches inside to get his reward, only to discover that with his fistful of candies he is stuck. He has two alternatives. He can either hang on to the candies and be captured, or he can let go and be free. What do the monkeys choose? They choose to hang on to the candy and be captured! *Even though the monkeys never get to eat the candies, they refuse to let go.* As a result, they surrender their life! The *illusion* of how good it would taste ultimately creates their demise.

When I read this story, I was struck by how many of us do the same thing. The constant illusion of the satisfaction that externals will bring us ultimately destroys the quality of our lives. It kills our chance to live life in a joyful manner. It's time that we released our hand and let go of the "candies" in order to be free to live a life that is truly worth living, a life that is filled with many exquisite moments.

4

FEEL THE FEAR AND
DON'T DO IT ANYWAY!

Don't just do something, stand there!
A "recovering" workaholic

I WROTE THE BOOK *FEEL THE Fear and Do It Anyway* for those many situations in life where "doing it" brings us great joy and satisfaction once we get past the fear. Perhaps the sequel could have been *Feel the Fear and **Don't** Do It Anyway*, for those situations where "not doing it" brings us great joy and satisfaction—once we get past the fear!

You may be asking yourself what can be fearful about NOT doing something. When it comes to the two addictions I discuss in this chapter—WORKAHOLISM (which includes our need to be busy all the time) and PERFECTIONISM—you will agree that NOT doing it is very difficult indeed. In order to end the struggle and dance with life, it is essential that we learn how to let go in these two areas. Let me point you in the right direction.

LET GO OF THE ADDICTION TO WORK

Workaholism, as I am using it here, is the obsessive need to be busy at the expense of a rich and balanced life. A workaholic lets this obsessive need override the importance of intimacy with family and friends, personal growth, quiet times, and the pleasure of play.

Workaholics include not only those in the workforce but also homemakers who feel they are never doing enough, retirees who compulsively get up at six in the morning to "work" on their hobbies, vacationers who appear to be playing but can't get their minds off of work or who are compelled to cram everything into those few precious days of freedom, and anyone who is driven to more-better-best. In all these cases,

The addiction of workaholism causes us to struggle with living!

Yet with all the damage that workaholism creates, it has strangely been called a "positive addiction." As the workaholic runs around avoiding the essence of life, the world applauds. It is the one addiction people even get to boast about! But is there such a thing as a positive addiction? Hardly! Since addictions *of any kind* are a product of the Lower Self, they create struggle and take away our peace.

There is little to mask the fact that workaholism is dysfunctional. Yet upon investigation, we find that workaholism is an addiction that is increasing in our society—and it can kill. Our hospitals are filled with people making themselves sick with their inability to take the time to rest their exhausted bodies and minds. A workaholic's vacation is often humorously—and sadly—depicted as a stay in the hospital. A workaholic friend of mine is actually looking forward to surgery, as it gives her an excuse to slow down for a while! Even more shocking is the case of a workaholic who, when told he was soon going to die, started to enjoy life for the first time he could remember. Why? He didn't have to struggle anymore! There is definitely something wrong with this picture.

Some people *think* they are handling their addiction to work by turning to the many antistress techniques that are available today. Even though I am a great fan of many of these techniques, in this case they don't get rid of the problem—overworking. They just give us more strength to keep working! Without treating the addiction, the anti-stress techniques offer false hope for a cure.

Why do any of us become workaholics? There are many strongly held beliefs as to why we work so hard. Upon scrutiny, however, these beliefs hold no truth. For example,

> Some of us believe that it is necessary to work, work, work, in order to be a success in life. Yet it is said that Albert Ein-

stein worked in the mornings and spent most of his afternoons sailing. I think most of us would agree that Einstein was successful! There are many other examples of successes in life who were not workaholics. So maybe it isn't necessary to be a workaholic in order to succeed in life.

Some of us believe that workaholism is conducive to good business practices. Yet studies show that compulsive, narrowly focused, competitive, tense individuals can't see the forest for the trees. Hence, creativity and productivity are hindered, not helped. So maybe our addiction to work has nothing to do with good business practices.

Some of us believe that it is necessary to be a workaholic in order to provide for our family. Yes, there are those, such as single parents, who are compelled to work hard to make ends meet. But they aren't necessarily workaholics. They work because of circumstances, not an unhealthy need. A workaholic is *driven to work*, even when there is enough money. So maybe our addiction to work hasn't anything to do with providing for our family.

Some of us believe one must be a workaholic in order to run a "proper home." Is a proper home a place where everything is spotless and rigidly managed? Or is it one that is filled with a sense of ease, flow, comfort, acceptance, and the peace of a relaxed person who is not driven to excesses of control? I'll take the latter any day! So maybe our addiction to work has nothing to do with running a "proper" home.

I could go on with popularly held, but erroneous, reasons why people are workaholics. But let me get to some of the *real* reasons people are workaholics. As I see it,

Workaholism is a fix. It is an escape. It allows us to turn the other way so that we don't have to come face to face with our inner pain, or our intense sense of emptiness, or

our lack of self-worth, or our need for an identity, or our drivenness to more-better-best, or our inability to have meaningful relationships, or our fear of not having enough or being enough.

Read this again. No wonder we want to escape! No wonder we want to mask our yearning for a life that means more than it does! What a raging whirlpool lies beneath the surface! When we who are workaholics are not absorbed in our work, we are forced to ask ourselves, "Who am I, what am I, why am I—if I am not busy, busy, busy, doing, doing, doing?" And, sadly, we are too frightened to explore the answer to these profound questions. As a result, we never get a chance to behold the magic and wonder and vastness of the unused parts of ourselves. Instead, it's calls to make, people to meet, projects to complete . . . busy, busy, busy.

And we feel so virtuous about it, not realizing that we are cheating ourselves and all those who are significant in our lives. To add insult to injury, despite all the work we do, we never feel "finished." There is always something more that "needs" to be done. Even when we are way ahead of schedule, we have the gnawing sense we are lagging behind or that we are missing opportunities that we should be creating or that we are not contacting people we should be contacting. Talk about stress!

How can we still those rough waters? How can we learn to feel at peace within ourselves? What are some steps we can take to pull ourselves out of our addiction to work? As I discussed earlier, the essence of the cure for any addiction is to pull ourselves out of the quagmire of the Lower Self and find the place of peace within our Higher Self.

An effective way of dealing with a multitude of addictions is to attend one of the twelve-step programs, all of which are based on Spiritual principles. Although each of these self-help programs is a separate entity, they are all derived from the original twelve-step program, Alcoholics Anonymous (AA). Today there are a whole host of other "anonymouses" dealing with codependency, drugs, gambling, sex, and so on. It is not surprising that there is now a twelve-step program called Workaholics Anonymous. For anyone on the treadmill of work, work, work, attending Workaholics Anonymous is one way to begin the healing process.[1]

Another way to begin the healing process is to incorporate Spiritual practices into our everyday lives. Again, Spiritual practices do not necessarily have any religious connotations. They pertain to those tools that help us feel connected to our Higher Self—our place of inner strength, inner power, and inner love. Many of these practices are described in my previous works and many more are included in Part III of this book. *The purpose of all these Spiritual practices is to bring the healing voice of the Higher Self into our consciousness as we drown out the destructive chatter of our Lower Self.* As our Higher Self becomes more dominant in our life, we are able to slow down and live a more balanced and rewarding life. Remember that . . .

The Lower Self punishes; the Higher Self rewards.

Why would anyone want to listen to the messages of the Lower Self?

Another important step in learning how to get rid of our workaholic tendencies is to learn how to say NO! As I discuss in Chapter 7, one of my favorite tools to end the struggle and dance with life is to "Say YES to the Universe." In this case, *say YES to saying NO!* Initially, saying NO to tasks brought before us can bring on great anxiety. That's okay! *FEEL THE FEAR AND SAY NO ANYWAY!* Very quickly, you will realize that our motivation for doing most of the tasks brought before us has less to do with the tasks than it has to do with making ourselves feel more important or more secure or more wanted. Ouch! As you break the self-destructive habit of taking on more than you can comfortably handle, you will breathe a sigh of relief!

In the same vein, look at your appointment schedule. Are all those appointments really necessary? Or if you are a housewife or househusband, is everything on that to-do list so important? I love this quote from Gore Vidal:

"There is nothing more debasing than the work of those who do well what is not worth doing at all."[2]

That should set you thinking! He is suggesting that we are humiliating ourselves by wasting our time on something that doesn't have to be done in the first place! Of course, if we are enjoying "doing well what is not worth doing it at all," then it can hardly be a waste of time. But if we are doing it out of obligation at the expense of balance in our lives, then we are selling ourselves short.

Another way to heal our workaholism is to learn how to delegate. As Jann Mitchell wisely advises us:

"Let go and let someone else."[3]

Most of us are very arrogant. We think there is only one way to do things—our way! When we hold onto the reins in this way, we weave a complicated web for ourselves. It would simplify life a great deal if we really did let go and let someone else—*in his or her own way*. This, of course, is not easy for us control freaks!

A colleague of mine who held an executive position was in a workaholic rut. Her problem was that she needed to feel that she was indispensable, and as a result, she held the reins much too tightly. Exhausting! One day she made a conscious decision to begin easing her hold on those reins. Slowly, she began delegating responsibilities she had been unnecessarily hoarding for herself. Yes, the letters that went out of the office were different from the ones she would have written. Yes, the food at the business parties would have been different if she had worked with the caterer. Yes, the staff would have been different if she had been doing all the hiring. And so on. But you know what? *It all worked anyway!*

This is a little hard to take in the beginning—that it can all work anyway, that you are not as "important" as you thought you were. But the advantages are enormous. By delegating, you allow others to give their gift to the world. By delegating, you can focus on the *real* reason you were hired. By delegating, you have more time to devote to family and friends. By delegating, you have the time to create a richer life—thus allowing you to be less emotionally dependent on your job.

Delegating on the job is no different from delegating at home. When you give tasks to your children, you give them the message that they are important, contributing members of your household. So many of our children seem arrogant and spoiled, and I believe that it is their lack of a sense of self that makes them behave so badly sometimes. Making them a meaningful part of the household creates in them a sense that their life makes a difference. Also, delegating tasks to children teaches them to be more independent. Just as important, you feel less resentful of your children when you are not so overworked. And you raise the level of *your* self-esteem knowing that you are worthy of help.

The benefits of delegating are enormous. The challenge is to learn how to turn over those tasks with some necessary instruction, then *get out of everyone's way.* Praise the work that has been done, even if it is not done the way you would have done it. For example, if you are always criticizing your children for the "wrong" choices they are making when doing the food shopping, they eventually will stop shopping! Remember there are no wrong choices; there are only different choices. There are only different ways of making a bed, or drying the dishes, or cleaning the garage, or whatever. Lighten up. Let go. I suggest you start this delegation process very slowly, with little tasks first. And as you do . . .

Practice letting go. Practice honoring someone else's efforts. Practice praising others for *their* way even if it's different from your way.

Soon you will have much more loving relationships with everyone around you!

At first, it's very frightening to alter our addictive need to work. We really believe that if we don't kill ourselves working, we won't have enough money, or we'll be lost in the shuffle, or others will think less of us, or whatever. Eventually, as we enter the realm of the

Higher Self, we discover what life is truly about. It's about love, beauty, grace, ease, appreciation, and all those things that make life more joyous.

Paradoxically, the more I have been able to relax and live a balanced life, the more productive I have become. More important, the quality of my life has improved enormously. I have even learned how to "waste" time doing things that have absolutely no purpose whatsoever except to bring me pleasure. In fact, I've come up with a new way of looking at "wasting time":

If you are not enjoying yourself, you are wasting your time!

Once in a while the obsessive need to work rears its ugly head. At such times I know that I am best served by sitting myself down in a quiet spot and figuring out what I am trying to mask with my constant activity. I always come up with an answer that leads the way to relief. Either I'm fearful about money, or I'm fearful I'm not good enough if I don't keep working, or whatever Lower-Self fear that it happens to be that day. I then pick up one of the many Spiritual tools available that take me out of the realm of my Lower Self and lift me to the realm of my Higher Self. Magic!

So the next time that compulsive desire to work comes upon you, FEEL THE FEAR AND *DON'T* DO IT ANYWAY! Sit yourself down in a quiet spot and reflect on your life. Ask yourself, "What am I trying to avoid with this constant busyness? What am I frightened to look at within myself? How can I make myself feel 'good enough?' How can I begin creating more balance and trust in my life? How can I fill the emptiness I feel when I am quiet?" Then listen. As you begin answering these important questions with all the masks stripped away, you can then use the many Spiritual tools available to you to heal any of the hurts or fears that have been controlling you.

Remember that a balanced life—one that is filled with the riches of play, intimacy with family and friends, alone time, personal growth, and so on—helps us feel abundant. When we feel abundant, our addiction to work falls by the wayside, which is where it belongs!

LET GO OF THE NEED TO BE PERFECT

Perfection is another crazy-making addiction. Our bodies have to be perfect. Our job performance has to be perfect. We have to be perfect mothers or fathers. We have to plan the party perfectly. We have to be the perfect boss. Our houses have to be cleaned perfectly. And on and on and on.

Are you perfect yet? Neither am I! *Nor will we ever be.* We are *all* human beings doing the very best we can. And human beings weren't born to be perfect.

We were born to learn, to grow, to expand, to love, to create, to enjoy, to see the beauty in all things—including ourselves. But we weren't born to be perfect!

Why then do so many of us focus on an impossible goal? Again, the quagmire of our Lower Self keeps us stuck in the idea that if we are not perfect, people will think less of us. It keeps us stuck in the idea that if we are not perfect, we are not good enough. This last point creates a real breakdown in logic:

In order to be good enough, we have to be perfect. Since no one is perfect, no one is good enough!

This makes no sense whatsoever. The truth is . . .

We are all good enough! And no one is perfect! Even the Buddhas have their days!

Hence our striving for perfection is one of the most useless, wasteful endeavors on which we spend our time. Even the most enlightened of us regularly trip and fall—and it's totally okay.

The need for perfection is often agonizingly painful. How many of us have felt deep within us a moan of frustration and exhaustion that results from our trying too hard? Or a moan of disappointment in ourselves for never reaching our goal of perfection? The frustration, exhaustion, and disappointment sometimes lead us to depression, even suicide. While most of us don't take it that far, our addiction to perfection certainly kills our enjoyment of life.

The reason our addiction to perfection can be so devastating is that we believe our self-worth is measured by our performance. But since no one is perfect, it is impossible to attain self-worth through perfection. Do I detect another ladder resting on the wrong wall?

How do we begin to change this self-destructive pattern? It helps to look, once again, at the power of ENOUGH in the context of our addiction to perfection. Here this wonderful word reminds us that when we have done our very best—win or lose—we have done enough, and we *are* enough. This Higher-Self reminder leads us to the place of peace and fulfillment.

Therefore, when the pangs of not good enough come creeping in from the voice of our Lower Self, simply drown it out with . . .

I am good enough.
I am good enough.
I am good enough.
I am good enough.
I am good enough.

Say it over and over again, until your enoughness seeps into the deepest recesses of your being. If you don't get that job you were hoping to get, you are good enough. If you spent a lot of time preparing your report and your boss criticizes, you are good enough. And so on.

Understand that the realization that you are good enough and that the results of your efforts are good enough is not an excuse to be sloppy and uncaring. It serves our sense of self to put a loving effort into whatever we do in life. But this loving effort needs to be totally detached from an addiction to perfection.

**Feelings of accomplishment and satisfaction do not come
from striving to be perfect. They do come from the
process of using our inner power, beauty, and love in a
creative, expansive, positive, and loving way.**

There is another time our need to be perfect gets in the way of
our enjoying life to the fullest. That is when we avoid doing something we've never tried before for fear we won't be good enough.
God forbid! We might make a fool of ourselves! For example, I've
seen too many people *not* get on that dance floor because they feel
they can't dance as well as the others on the floor. They are missing
out on a wonderful time! I love Linda Weltner's motto:

"Anything worth doing is worth doing badly."[4]

Understand the great wisdom in her humor. We have been taught
that we should go for excellence in anything we attempt. We are
afraid of making a fool of ourselves (whatever that means!). Therefore, if we don't do it really well, we don't have a good time. Or
we refrain from doing it at all. We must keep reminding ourselves,
that . . .

Our goal is to enjoy, not to achieve perfection!

If it's worth doing and you're having a great time doing it, who cares
if you are doing it well or not?

So you see that in order to end the struggle and dance with life
we must learn to make enjoyment, not perfection, our goal. This
movement of the ladder to a different wall makes the difference between a life lived with a joyous Spirit or one that is lived with pun-
ishing self-doubt.

And, remember, if someone points out your "ineptness" in any
given endeavor, simply say, "I'm doing good enough," and then go
on to have the best time you ever had!

ENJOY! ENJOY! ENJOY!

5

DROP THE HEAVY BAGGAGE

I lead a very simple life, yet some nights I cannot sleep because I am so excited about the next day. I find joy and laughter in everything I do.

Sheila Byrd

S HEILA BYRD WROTE ME A FAN letter. But I have become one of her fans. She is sixty-eight years old and despite her very hard life, she radiates joy. Sheila was married to an alcoholic who left when their daughter was young. She has little money. Her daughter is having many difficulties dealing with her own life. But somehow, through it all, Sheila has learned to capture the essence of life rather than the shadow. She has learned to transcend the smallness of the Lower Self and enter the world of the Higher Self where the picture of life is grand.

When I first read her letter, I was struck with the words, "I lead a very simple life." I thought about the lightness in her attitude that matched her simple life. It reminded me that so many of us have lost the art of simplicity. And, believe me, it is an art! Life has become excruciatingly complicated, cluttered, heavy, and joyless. Hardly a model for ending the struggle and dancing with life!

How do we simplify? How do we let go of some of the excess baggage that we carry around with us? Our collection of physical and emotional clutter makes us feel as though we are going through life carrying a watermelon and an overloaded suitcase! It's time to drop these tremendous weights and learn how to live in the freedom that simplicity allows. Let me show you how you can begin lightening the load in a number of areas of your life. As you read, think of other excess baggage you've been carrying around as well. It's definitely time to LET GO!

CUT THE CORD

One of the biggest weights we carry around with us has to do with our need to control other people in our lives. In this regard, I find the following quote from an unknown sage extremely enlightening:

> "Never try to teach a pig to sing. It wastes your time and it annoys the pig."

Don't get me wrong! It's not that people in our life are pigs. It's that we waste an incredible amount of time in our futile attempts to make others into something they're definitely not! Whether it's about changing the thoughts and actions of our wives, husbands, children, parents, siblings, friends, or whomever, we are barking up the wrong tree.

When we try to change people, which is the same thing as controlling them, we are going against the grain—the essence—of who they are at this point in their lives. We are blind to the fact that they have their own Journey, their own lessons to learn, their own capabilities, their own purpose. They were brought into this world with a different agenda from ours. Therefore, it is wise to get out of their way and let them become who they are meant to become.

A friend of mine was terribly upset because her eighteen-year-old daughter had gotten a tattoo on her arm. She felt that with a tattoo, her daughter wouldn't be accepted, or wouldn't find a good husband, or would be considered bizarre, and so on. Her daughter, of course, was upset that her mother didn't mind her own business! A major battle between the two egos developed.

I said to my friend, "Why don't you just trust that your daughter has her own road to travel, her own lessons to learn. Why get in the way? Why not ask yourself why a tattoo on your daughter's arm is *really* bothering you so much?" I explained that that was a much more powerful way of handling the situation than berating her daughter and upsetting herself.

In the same vein, it would have been wonderful if someone had asked her daughter, "Why are you so dependent on the opinions and approval of your mother? Instead of screaming at her, why don't you ask yourself why you couldn't just respond calmly, 'Thanks for caring, Mom, but I have to follow my own path, not yours.'"

This situation is a good demonstration of what has come to be known as codependency. For the purposes of this book, codependency is an inability to establish healthy boundaries between ourselves and others. As a result *their* behavior determines *our* self-esteem, happiness, and sense of peace and flow. By definition, this inability to establish boundaries sets up an addictive need to control other people's behavior. We *must* try to control their behavior since we can't control our own! Unfortunately, this is an exercise in futility!

What could be some of the *real* reasons my friend was so upset? Perhaps she was afraid that others would judge *her* badly if her daughter had a tattoo. Perhaps she felt she was no longer needed by her daughter who made decisions about her life on her own. Perhaps she felt guilty that she wasn't the "perfect" mother who raised the "perfect" child (according to her idea about what was perfection). Perhaps she had no trust in her daughter's ability to handle the consequences of her actions. These are difficult issues to look at; it was much easier to lash out at her daughter's behavior rather than look at her *reactions* to her daughter's behavior. It is, of course, only by looking at her reactions that the real answers to her upset can be found.

Naturally, it is much easier to look inside when the problem concerns something relatively minor: What if the problem involves an alcoholic mate, a child flunking out of school, a parent who has always been righteous, critical, and unloving? These more serious issues make it an even bigger challenge to create proper boundaries. Nevertheless, it is essential that we do create these boundaries.

Bob's nineteen-year-old son was taking drugs and flunking out of college. Bob was brought up believing that he was responsible for everyone around him, that everyone else's happiness (or unhappiness) depended on him. He also believed that he could somehow change others with his words, actions, or attitudes. So at the beginning of his son's troubling times, Bob desperately tried to "fix" his son, but to no avail.

Eventually, he realized his powerlessness in this situation. He had to pull back entirely and let his son find his own way. This was very difficult, but at the same time, very freeing. He said he asked God to take over and give his son what was needed for his highest good. With that, he bowed out of the picture and let God take over.

His son dropped out of school and lived a very paltry kind of existence, but Bob no longer was an enabler, which in codependency terms means someone who tries to shield another from the harmful consequences of his or her behavior. This sounds noble, but it ultimately is controlling and destructive, as the other person is allowed to continue irresponsible behavior. Instead, Bob used what has come to be known as tough love.

If Bob had continued to be an enabler he would have given his son money, bailed him out of any trouble he got himself into, made excuses for his behavior, attempted to control all situations in his son's life, made threats to his son that he didn't have the courage to carry out, blamed himself or others for his son's problems, and so on. Instead he chose to let go and trust the Grand Design of his son's life. It took a while, six years to be exact, but eventually his son awakened to the possibility of a more satisfying and productive life. He now walks a healthier and more responsible path than he walked before. And for the first time, Bob and his son have a chance at being friends.

Someone asked Bob how he would have felt if his son had ended up dead or in prison. His answer was, "I did the best I could. I tried to get him help, but to no avail. Finally, I simply had to let go. If he ended up dead or in prison, it would have been incredibly painful, but I would have known that it wasn't my fault. That was his choice. While I would have mourned the loss, I would not have let the quality of my life depend on his decisions in life." Enabling behavior doesn't help another person; it makes matters worse. Bob's method of tough love was the healthiest thing he could have done for himself and his son, despite the ultimate outcome.

If you feel you can't react to some situation in your life with the strength that Bob showed when it came to his son's predicament, do attend the twelve-step program called Co-Dependents Anonymous.[1] The Higher-Self principles you will learn there will be invaluable to your life—and to the lives of those you are trying to control.

There are many other kinds of groups that you can join, such as self-help groups and therapist-led groups. I firmly believe in the group process. It is important to have the support of caring, like-minded people when you are going through difficult times. Understand that there are healthy groups and unhealthy groups, which I discuss in detail in *Dare to Connect*.[2] It's important to know the difference! Most important, if the group fosters a victim mentality, run the other way! You want a group that fosters a loving and powerful approach to living.

There are also many tools you can use on your own. For example, the following image is wonderful for helping you cut codependent attachments.

Close your eyes. Relax your body. In your mind's eye, see the person you are trying to control or change standing in front of you. Imagine an umbilical cord holding the two of you together so that when one moves, the other has to move. Feel the discomfort, pain, and sense of imprisonment this attachment creates. Not a great environment for ending the struggle and dancing with life!

Now, in your mind's eye, see yourself picking up huge scissors and cutting the cord. Feel the instant relief, freedom, and peace this allows. Take a deep breath and notice how you've set *both of you* free. Move around and notice that the other person is not forced to move with you. And notice that when the other person moves, you are free to stand on your own, tall and whole.

Repeat this powerful visualization every time you are tempted to run someone else's life. Or if you are allowing someone to run yours, which is the other side of the same coin.

Sometimes those with whom we are codependent don't really want to be set free, as they imagine their survival to be tied up with their connection to us. We have to assure them of our love and communicate our trust that they will have the strength to handle their own lives. As far as I am concerned, this is the ultimate in loving—*caring, but not controlling.* Unconditional love means standing back and trusting those we love to follow their own path, *despite the outcome,* without our judgment, righteousness, and anger. Of course, when children are young, guidance and appropriate discipline are necessary. Of course, there is a place for our being there for others in the role of friend, coach, or model. But being a crutch or critic doesn't serve anyone.

In the end, we have to stop using other people to fill us up. We need to create our own happiness by detaching from our dependency on others. If peace in your heart is dependent on how other people are going to act, you are living in the realm of the Lower Self and you will constantly be in conflict. As you cut that cord, you are free to live in the realm of the Higher Self where your happiness is dependent only on the realization that you are a powerful and loving person who has much to give to this world.

DROP THE SHOULDS AND SHOULDN'TS

Another bit of sage advice you might have heard recently is, "Don't 'should' on me!" I would add, "Don't 'should' on yourself, either!" So much of the weight of our lives comes from the huge amount of

"shoulds" and "shouldn'ts" others try to impose on us and, ultimately, those we impose on ourselves. To name a few . . .

I should exercise at least a half hour a day.
I should send my children to the best schools.
I should answer all my mail.
I should pick up the phone every time it rings.
I should be the perfect host (or hostess).
I should make lots of money.

Shoulds and shouldn'ts are signs of our need to conform. It is
better if we learn to follow our heart, to follow our instinct about
the way life is best lived for who we are as human beings.

For example, Janet was always dreading the Christmas season
because she hated to send Christmas cards. It seemed like such a
chore. One day she asked herself, "Why am I doing this when it
weighs so much on my mind and on my time?"

The following Christmas she decided to stop sending Christmas
cards. What a relief! She reported that to her knowledge no one
even noticed! Her friends have remained her friends. Her business
acquaintances are just as cooperative as ever. Friends with whom
she truly wants to connect get a phone call that says, "I love you and
wish you all wonderful things for this holiday season." Her holiday
season has become so much easier and so much freer since she
doesn't feel obligated to send those cards. Of course there are many
who *love* to send Christmas cards and they definitely will want to
continue to do so. But when sending cards becomes an obligation
instead of a joy, it's definitely time to stop.

Does Janet enjoy getting cards? Of course, she does. But she
doesn't think any less of people who don't send her a card. In fact,
she reports sometimes being put off by cards with printed names and
no personalization. She feels the senders are sending them because
it is a should in their life, not a genuine act of caring.

As an exercise, write down as many shoulds and shouldn'ts you can think of that have become a chore instead of a joy. Now cross them off your list one at a time. For example, you don't have to make your bed every day . . . unless you *want* to. You don't have to have a clean car . . . unless you *want* to. My friend has actually replaced the flowers in his garden with painted wooden flowers so he doesn't have to water them anymore! You get the idea.

Shoulds that come from the Lower Self fragment our lives. They make us worry. They make us do too much, think too much, plan too much. These shoulds pull us apart and make us lose our center. Remember that from a Higher-Self perspective, our enjoyment and contribution to life come from following our own heart, and everyone's heart is different. Simply ask your Higher Self what is right for you to do relative to your particular purpose here on earth and listen for the response. This is being your own person. This is being the best that you can be.

Sometimes we are called upon to do things for others, such as bringing food to a sick relative, and sometimes we may not be in the mood to do these things for others, which causes us to feel resentful. Resentment is a Lower-Self emotion. When we move beyond the Lower Self and enter the realm of the Higher Self, our resentment disappears as we understand the contribution we are making to someone else's life. From this perspective, we become infused with an energy of love and caring. Our life is enriched instead of diminished. In this way, our "should" is transformed into a "want to."

Sometimes we are required to pay the bills, wash the dishes, drive our children to school, and other such everyday activities. Again, we may not be in the mood, which brings up feelings of resentment. Here, too, we can move beyond the Lower Self and enter the realm of the Higher Self by focusing on the give-and-take of life. We pay our bills understanding that we have taken goods and services that belong to others and it is now time to return the favor. We wash the dishes grateful for the food we have eaten. We drive our children to school thankful that they are in our lives (and that someone else will be taking care of them for a few hours!). From this higher perspective, we begin to see the gifts inherent in everything we do. And, once again, our "should" can be transformed into a "want to."

LET GO OF THE NEED TO "KNOW IT ALL"

I'm a "recovering know-it-all," and I *know* just how painful and disempowering this need to impress everyone with my incredible knowledge can be! I read with embarrassment the following quote of Lao Tzu:

> "To know that you do not know is the best. To pretend to know when you do not know is disease."

Ouch! Recently I have learned that . . .

From the level of the Lower Self, not knowing is stupidity; from the level of the Higher Self, not knowing is great wisdom!

Thank goodness I'm learning more and more how to be in the presence of my Higher Self! From here, not knowing signifies a clear and open mind. It signifies that there is enough room left to expand and grow, that I haven't cluttered my mind with hardened matter, that I'm free to let go and to receive. Merciful abundance!

The truth is that we know very little. To pretend otherwise is a sign of great insecurity. We think we should know, so we trick ourselves into believing we actually do know everything. Yet these are times of rapid change. It is reported that the pace of change is five times what it was fifty years ago. In addition, it is estimated that our information load doubles every seven years. Who can keep up? NO ONE! While some pretend to, they are living a lie. While some try to, they are creating unnecessary stress in their lives.

When I was addicted to knowing it all, I was always afraid I was missing something I should know. So I coveted newspapers, magazines, and books. I was afraid to throw anything away. Now that I'm on my way to "recovery," I know that I am *definitely* missing something—and that's perfectly okay. I actually throw or give away a lot of newspapers, magazines, and books without even opening them. What a relief!

Also, we know-it-alls think we know how people are supposed to act, how they are supposed to raise their children, how they are supposed to diet, how they are supposed to pray, how they are supposed to conduct themselves sexually, how they are supposed to think, and on and on and on. Oh, how we fool ourselves!

You may be asking, "But what about opinions? Aren't we allowed to have opinions?" Barry Stevens tells us that the Jains in India have the word *syat*, which means "to the best of my knowledge at this time." They toss it into conversation frequently to remind themselves and others that that is all anyone has to go on.[3]

A wonderful exercise is to practice saying "I don't know" to others when they ask your opinion. Or adapt the Jain word *syat*—"to the best of my knowledge at this time, I think that . . ." You might want to end with, "but I don't know how I will feel tomorrow." That's open. That's freeing. That's also the truth!

These are just a few pieces of emotional baggage for you to work on. I know it only scratches the surface, but you get the picture. If you look long enough and hard enough, you realize that all your negative emotions—including anger, blame, guilt, low self-esteem, and fear—signal that you are stuck in the clutches of your Lower Self and you need to extricate yourself so that you can reconnect with your Spiritual "Home," your Higher Self. In this way, your negative emotions actually serve a valuable function. When you heed the signal and reconnect with your Higher Self, you find that these negative emotions fall by the wayside and peace is mercifully restored within your being.

So anytime you find yourself laden down with negative feelings of any kind, ask yourself,

"What would my Higher Self say about all this?"

As your access to the Higher Self becomes easier and easier, you begin to see all things in your life in a much more loving and powerful way. The relief is enormous!

DROP THE EXCESS PHYSICAL BAGGAGE

As I discussed earlier, we live in a society that encourages accumulation. We have been taught that more is definitely better! As a result, we always seem to hang on to more than we actually need. This is heavy baggage! You may think that excessive accumulation is a characteristic only of the rich. Not so! I have visited many homes of rich and poor alike and am struck by the excess of "things" that seem to be everywhere.

My home is no exception. My husband and I had to vacate our house for three months so that some major renovations could be done. The condominium we rented for those three months had tiny closets, a big contrast to the large walk-in closet that I was used to. Since I couldn't take many clothes with me, I carefully packed a limited wardrobe that I hoped would carry me through.

When I finished packing, I looked at the remaining clothes that were to go into storage and was shocked to realize that the closet looked as full as when I started to pack. Hardly a dent was made! I said, "Something is definitely wrong with this picture." As the three months wore on, I was further amazed when *I didn't wear half of the very limited supply of clothes I had brought with me!* I had to ask myself what all this accumulation was about.

When I returned home, I set about the task of getting rid of clothes I had not worn for at least a year. I was surprised that this wasn't as easy as I expected. I found myself hanging on as if those clothes were a matter of life and death, which they obviously weren't since I hadn't worn them in over a year. I even had difficulty giving away a belt I hadn't worn in ten years! I kept thinking that maybe I would find a great use for it. Who was I kidding? I hadn't been thin enough to wear it for at least eight of those ten years! I had forgotten I even had it! What was I hanging on to? In the deep recesses of my Lower Self, I knew the answer to that question.

Many of us who hang onto clutter or unused possessions are afflicted with a poverty consciousness. We feel, at some level of our being, that there isn't enough—enough clothes, enough furniture, enough money, enough love, enough praise. (There's that magical word again, ENOUGH.) I am sure that this is part of my need to hang on.

If you suspect that you, too, hang on to things because of a poverty consciousness, then I suggest you do as I did. Keep repeating to yourself the following words as you begin letting go of the clutter in your life:

I have enough. I am letting go.
I have enough. I am letting go.
I have enough. I am letting go.

As you keep repeating these two important thoughts, you will feel the grasp of your addiction to hanging on to the excesses in your life begin to loosen and a feeling of lightness overtaking you. *Constant repetition of these affirmations is important.* As you know, old habits are hard to break, even when they make absolutely no sense whatsoever.

It also helps to think of yourself as part of the flow of life. As you donate your excess clothes and dishes and furniture to others who truly do *need* what is excessive in your life, you realize that you have made someone else's life a little easier. You have become a source of abundance to them. This is hugely gratifying.

I suggest you go through the closets, drawers, and cabinets in your home and office and begin the process of letting go. What will you find there?

Books you will never read again, clothes you will never wear again, audiotapes you will never listen to again, cosmetics you will never put on your face again, pots you will never cook in again, files that you will never open again—and much more.

In the beginning, it is difficult letting go. But as you get into the swing of it, you will feel lighter and fresher and better able to see what you *really* need. This is what I imagine spring cleaning is truly about.

You may be asking, "Why, in the grand scope of life, is cleaning our closets so important? What's the big deal?" Well, I'll tell you. It creates a trickle-down of relief: As you get rid of the excess, you begin to realize:

You don't need (or want!) as much as you thought you did, which means . . .

You don't need to buy as many things, which means . . .

You don't need as much space, which means . . .

You don't need to have a bigger house, which means . . .

You don't need to earn as much, which means . . .

You don't need to work so hard, which means . . .

You have more time and energy, which means . . .

You are able to lessen the struggle and dance with life!

It's amazing how far a good cleaning of your closets will take you, isn't it? I'll bet you feel lighter just thinking about it!

There is something else to consider. Many of us yearn for more money thinking it will make our life much easier. And for those who are talking about money for survival—food, clothing, housing, schooling, and the like—this is true. But for those who are addicted to more-better-best, their accumulation of excesses makes them prisoners of responsibility. They have big cars, big houses, masses of belongings. They spend enormous amounts of money insuring and protecting their possessions. They work so hard on the upkeep of their lives that they have little time for pleasure and play. I watch many of these people struggling to relax! Their lives are not light and free. Their self-created burdens are very heavy indeed.

Again, this frantic lifestyle comes from a poverty consciousness that lurks deep within their being. It comes from their need to control and dominate. It comes from a deep feeling of insecurity. It's hard to imagine that many wealthy people have an intense poverty consciousness, but they do! When you ask them how they are, you get a barrage of "Woe is me!" instead of joy. I refer to them as "the affluent poor."

I was struck by a book title, *Your Money or Your Life*.[4] Sometimes that's exactly the choice we have to make. There are many who have made a good living, but they haven't made a good life. Again, with the right attitude, it can be comforting to have lots of money, and it's wonderful to have the choices that money allows. But when we are addicted to accumulation, we give up all that is wonderful about living.

This concept of lightening the load has had such an impact on my husband and me that we are selling our present home and moving into one that is smaller and simpler, one that allows us more freedom to dance with life. I totally understand what Ann Richards, ex-governor of Texas, meant when she said,

> "When I don't live in the mansion anymore, I want to live in the smallest house I can find."[5]

Richards understood the need of letting go of excess baggage. She called it *"discarding the distractions."* I like that! Anything that takes away our lightness and simplicity in living is definitely a distraction. So make a game out of it and discard as many distractions as you can in your home and office. My rule is this:

Use and enjoy that which enriches your life. Let go of that which is just excess baggage.

As you get rid of the excess baggage, you will learn that bigger is not always better. In this context, smaller, lighter, and less is definitely better! We talk in this country of raising our standard of living. There are times when *raising our standard of living actually lowers it!* When we are consumed with accumulating more-better-best from the external world, we lose more than we gain. I'm left with the conclusion that . . .

Raising our standard of living is truly about needing less and enjoying more!

Needing less and enjoying more is an appealing alternative for so many of us. But you already know that this is easier said than done. Later in the book, I introduce some wonderful ways to help you need less and enjoy more. For now, let me inspire you with the following story:

> There was a sixteenth-century Zen monk who was very poor and lived in a little hut on a mountainside. One night he came home to find a burglar in his hut. Knowing there was nothing much to take, he said to the thief, "I don't have much, but I would like to give you something." He then took off his clothes and gave them to the thief. Totally surprised by the monk's actions, the thief grabbed the clothes and ran out the door. Did the monk feel poor because of his loss? No. He sat there looking at the beauty of the night and said to himself, sadly, "I wish he would have stayed around a little longer. I could have given him the stars."

This Zen monk had found the essence of a life well lived. He didn't need to accumulate. He didn't need to control or judge the behavior of the thief. He wasn't laden with negative emotions of blame, anger, and fear. He didn't see himself as a victim (a "robbery survivor"!) He had mastered the art of living in the Higher-Self dimensions of abundance and beauty. He felt very rich.

I've never met anyone who has achieved such an advanced level of enlightment. I suspect you haven't either. Yet we all have our moments, the exquisite moments when we truly can let go and embrace the stars. During these moments of the sublime, nothing seems very important on the physical plane. All that's worth attaining seems to be on the Spiritual plane.

It stands to reason that the way to end the struggle and dance with life is to give conscious attention to the practice of releasing the scarcity of the Lower Self and embracing the abundance that lies in the highest part of who you are—your Higher Self. When you dwell in this magical place, you will learn all you ever need to know about ending the struggle and dancing with life.

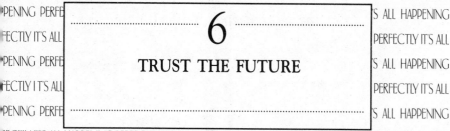

6

TRUST THE FUTURE

BARRY STEVENS HAS PUT HER
finger on one of the most important areas of our life that need
release—our expectations about the way things are "supposed
to" be (which you'll recognize as another variation of the shoulds
in our lives). We set our hearts on so many things—on a beautiful day for our garden party, on our children growing up to be the
way we want them to be, on making lots of money from our investments, on being married "until death do us part," and on and on
and on.

Sometimes things work out the way we expect them to, and
sometimes they don't. Whether they do or whether they don't,
holding on to expectations creates an enormous amount of worry,
conflict, and struggle.

We diminish the present as we worry about the future.

We don't enjoy the preparation for our outdoor party as we con-
cern ourselves about the weather. We don't enjoy the miracle of our
children's growth as we worry about how they will turn out. We
don't enjoy the abundance in our lives now as we worry about the
future of our investments. We twist ourselves all out of shape to
please our mate so that our marriage will last "until death do us

part." In essence, we lose the freedom to soar that comes from enjoying the vast riches that life has to offer in the here and now.

What if you knew your life would work beautifully even if it rained the day of the party, even if your children didn't turn out the way you hoped, even if you lost money in your investments, even if your marriage didn't last? When we let go of our expectations about events in our life being a certain way, we can allow ourselves the peaceful thought that it's all happening perfectly no matter how it turns out.

You can see how important it is for you to learn how to unset your heart. By definition,

Setting your heart on something is entering into a state of rigidity. Unsetting your heart is entering a state of flow.

I am often asked, "How can you set any goals in life without having expectations?" This is my answer in a nutshell:

Set as many goals as you want. Picture exactly what you would like to happen. With loving effort, do the work necessary to bring the desired results to fruition. And when you are satisfied that you have done as much as you can, LET GO OF THE OUTCOME!

In this way, you release any expectation about how it all will turn out. You relax into the flow of life's adventure knowing that in the grand scheme of things, life truly is happening perfectly. As John Lubbock wisely stated,

"When we have done our best, we should await the results in peace."

The truth is that we are not capable of seeing beyond our limited vision and into the grand possibilities that life has to offer. Sometimes when things don't turn out as we want them to, we are later shown how they really did turn out perfectly for our highest good. Either we learned a valuable lesson or a better opportunity presented itself. Let me show you how this works.

Imagine that you are angry because you didn't get the job you were hoping to get. It doesn't seem fair that someone who was not as qualified as you got the job instead. In addition to being angry, you are worried about what this means for your future success. Your Lower Self is giving you messages of gloom and doom and telling you over and over again, "You're not good enough to succeed." Heavy baggage indeed!

It's at this time that you need to remind yourself that you have two choices. One is to let this incident destroy your peace of mind and keep weighing you down. Then not only didn't you get the job, you also made yourself miserable! The other alternative is to *turn it over* to the wisdom within, your Higher Self, with the instruction:

Take over now. I trust there is a good reason for my not getting the job. And I trust this outcome was for my highest good. I trust you will tell me exactly what I need to know and exactly what I need to do about this situation.

When I say "turn it over," I mean TURN IT OVER. And when I say "trust," I mean TRUST! My own experiences in life have convinced me that things happen in our lives for very good reasons. Our very limited minds may not understand it all, but the Spiritual part of who we are understands perfectly. So when doubt comes creeping in, as it always will, it serves our peace of mind to keep repeating to ourselves over and over again that wonderful affirmation I introduced you to earlier:

IT'S ALL HAPPENING PERFECTLY!

If you focus on the learning and the growing instead of the anger and the fear, you lighten up. Life becomes simpler. The reason things happen the way they do unfolds just in the process of living itself. Remember:

While none of us understands the Grand Design, we can commit to using all our experiences, good or bad, as the

building blocks of a powerful and loving life. Then it is, indeed, all happening perfectly!

Once you have turned it over to your Higher Self, you then pay attention to the messages you are given through your intuition, which gives you valuable messages from the wisdom within. And you use the many Spiritual tools available today to quiet the mind so that you are able to hear what is the powerful and loving way to go in any situation in your life. With the enormous peace of mind that the thought "it's all happening perfectly" gives you, you move forward with the assurance that there is a meaning and purpose to it all.

In the example of your not getting the job you wanted, you may later find a job that is far better suited to who you are as an individual. Had you gotten the first job, you would have missed out on a wonderful opportunity! Or you may decide that something is lacking in your interview skills. So you get some instruction in this area. You are then much better prepared for the next job interview that comes your way. In addition, if you have created a very rich life for yourself, as I suggested in Chapter 4, then you will notice that the disappointment of not getting the job will be diminished. After all, *you are more than your job.* Your job is not your life; it is only a part of your life.

A popular sentiment in recent years is . . .

Be careful what you ask for. You might get it!

Since we don't know in our logical mind what is for our highest good, we indeed have to be very careful about what we ask for. The job that we asked for might turn out to be the proverbial job from hell! The mate we asked for might be the mate from hell! And so on.

When I don't get something I had been setting my sights on, I have learned to remind myself that obviously something else will come along that will be for my highest good. This wasn't it. And I stop hanging on to any disappointment I had. If I don't remind myself of this higher possibility, I suffer much unnecessary pain when things don't work out as I had planned.

I know all of this is easier said than done. The fear that exists in the realm of the Lower Self will pop up over and over again. And you will need to reassure yourself over and over again that "*all is well*." Ironically, when our negative emotions seem to be at their worst, that is, when we are most needy of a connection with our Higher Self, our distress makes us forget that this amazing source of power and love exists. Therefore, we need to find ways of *staying conscious* of the fact that we have drifted far from Home and simply need to find our way back again.

We stay conscious by developing *daily* practices that serve as constant reminders (which is what the next section of the book is all about). When incorporated into everyday life, these practices lighten everything we do. When you learn to unset your heart in this way, you have learned the secret of flowing with the energy of the Universe, of ending the struggle and dancing with life.

It is said that life is what happens when we've made other plans. If this is so, and we all know it is, then it doesn't make much sense to keep demanding that life be a certain way. It doesn't make much sense to go through life traveling down the same tunnel of expectation when we know that tunnel often brings us disappointment. It is an act of self-love to stop hanging on to the way it is supposed to be. It is this hanging on that causes us to be buffeted about by the unwelcome surprises in our life.

Again, the reason why setting your heart on anything is such a painful choice is that the need to control all the people and events of our life is a need of the Lower Self. In the world of the Lower Self, the future is *always* a scary place because of the terrifying feeling that we do not have the power to handle whatever happens to us. Therefore, the Lower Self needs a guarantee. But there are no guarantees in the outside world.

When we jump to the level of the Higher Self, we are greatly relieved to find the guarantee that we have been looking for. And that guarantee is:

NO MATTER WHAT LIFE DECIDES TO HAND ME, I'LL HANDLE IT!

That's a pretty powerful guarantee! Do you see the peace this assurance of our inner power brings us? No matter what life decides to hand us, we will be able to handle it! We can *never* control life in any other way. Yes, life is filled with surprises. But with the inner knowing that we can handle anything life hands us, we don't have to worry about the future any longer. We can get on with our life with a feeling of freedom and adventure. We can even begin to enjoy the mysteries, instead of feeling threatened by them. Wherever life takes us, we'll be okay!

Hence, it is clear that if we don't take the steps necessary to transcend the realm of the Lower Self, we will always live in a world of fear and with an understandable addiction to control. When we jump to the level of the Higher Self, our addiction to control releases. We let go of the reins and enjoy the ride—*wherever it's taking us*.

To help you get in touch with what it feels like to let go of your resistance to life, visualize the following over and over again. You might want to repeat it slowly into a tape recorder and listen to it with your eyes closed. It provides a very healing image.

Imagine yourself standing at the edge of a beautiful flowing river in the middle of a rich green valley. You're curious as to where the river is flowing. You decide that it's time to find out. A sturdy-looking rowboat sits at the side of this wonderful flowing river. How handy! You climb right in and then notice that there aren't any oars. Feeling a sense of safety and adventure, you know that you don't need any oars, that you are going to let the boat take you where it wants to go. You climb in, untie the rope that holds the boat to the shore, and your Journey begins. You sit up tall and eager, determined to enjoy the Journey, no matter where it takes you. You take a deep breath and relax as you feel the boat drawn into the flow of the river. Knowing you have no control over where you are going, you say to yourself, "I let go and allow the river to carry me to new adventures. I trust that I am safe." Just feel the freedom as the boat carries you forward. You know you will hit bumpy times and you know you will hit times of great calm. They are all part of the Journey. You know you will enjoy the mystery of wherever your sturdy boat is taking you. And you know that when the Journey is over, you will be glad to have tasted it all.

What a beautiful image! In so many ways, our life is like that Journey. We've all been born as passengers. Time is taking us—body, mind, and Soul—to new places every moment of every day. And we have to develop the trust that our little boat—our Higher Self—knows the way. My little boat has certainly taken me down pathways I never could have found by myself. The more I allow myself to tune into my Higher Self for guidance, the more my need to control the future disappears, and the more wonderful this Journey called life becomes.

Developing this kind of trust requires our *constantly* using our Spiritual tools. Even when we think we have the hang of it, new situations arise that bring up our need to control. But the more we find ways of dwelling in the house of our Higher Self and trusting the Grand Design, the easier it is for us to let go of our need to control.

I'm often asked how it can all be happening perfectly in a world of wars, fires, earthquakes, killing, and on and on (all of which I talk about in Chapter 8). My answer is one that I've learned to use a lot recently: "I don't know." But what I do know is that our human minds are not capable of understanding the Grand Design. I don't know the larger dimensions of the Universe that are beyond my grasp as an ordinary mortal. What I have been learning to do is simply *trust*.

There have been many times when I haven't understood why certain things have happened in my life. Much later, however, the great miracle of it all was revealed to me. I didn't understand why my first marriage didn't work out; I later learned that there was much I had to learn about becoming whole, and, for me, being on my own was a necessary step.[2] I didn't understand why I got cancer;

I later learned how much a life-threatening illness teaches us about enjoying life in the present.

So I have decided to work on trusting that there are reasons for all that is happening on this earth to each and every one of us. I may never understand what these reasons are, but that is irrelevant. *When trust is there, explanations are unnecessary.* I have been humbled by the miracles I have seen all around me; I no longer have to know all the whys. I have accepted the fact that there is so much I don't know. There is so much I will never know. So when your Lower Self asks "Why?" just say to it,

I don't know, but I trust it's all happening perfectly. It's all part of the Grand Design.

As I said earlier, letting the boat carry us down the river does not mean simply sitting at home waiting for life to happen. It certainly is up to us to take some action. We can begin taking more appropriate action in life when we learn how to listen to our innate intelligence, our intuition. Whether we are aware of it or not, the Higher Self is constantly sending us valuable messages that can guide us to where we need to go for our highest good. Our task is to learn how to tune in to these messages. Again, I give you many ways of tuning into this channel of great wisdom in the second half of the book. It is appropriate here to explain why the intuitive mind is so important.

In Western society, we are taught to think logically, not intuitively. Logical thinking is very important. It helps us get through our everyday mortal existence. For example, it helps us know that two plus two equals four, an essential concept to understand when we are paying our bills! But logical thinking is very limited. It uses only part of our brain.

When we add intuitive thinking to logical thinking, we expand enormously our inherent capability of living life in an incredibly powerful manner. We realize that we have available to us much more wisdom and guidance than we thought we had. The logical mind draws on the teachings of the physical plane; the intuitive mind draws on the teachings of the Spiritual plane. When the two are combined, our resources for guiding us into the future are unlimited. We certainly are much more than we thought we were!

Since we have not been trained to use the intuitive part of who we are, the question is, "How do we tune in to these powerful messages that are coming through to us?" The *Course in Miracles* suggested to me a good beginning. Every morning as you contemplate your day, ask your Higher Self three questions:

Where would you have me go?
What would you have me do?
What would you have me say, and to whom?[3]

Ask these questions with a sense of trust that your inner wisdom and power will come forth. Then consciously turn it over and go about your day. As your day progresses, listen to any inner messages that you are given. These are messages from the intuitive mind. Then start going where your energy wants to take you. Sometimes you just get the urge to call a friend, or a business contact, or whatever. That urge is your intuition speaking. Again, see where these urges are taking you.

In the beginning you may hear nothing. But eventually you will pick up on the guidance coming through. Some of it may make no sense to you consciously. But it will make sense to your Higher Self. Trust that. I have found that when I listen to my intuition, I am led to places that I would have never gone had I listened only to the logic of my rational mind. And the results have been magical. Let me recount the following story that I told in *Feel the Fear and Do It Anyway*. It has great relevance here.

My introduction to teaching and, ultimately, writing came about as a result of my listening to my intuition. At the time, I had a vague notion that I wanted to teach a course on fear. I put it off indefinitely, largely because I was too busy with my job as an administrator to write up the course description and outline and then find the school that would want me to teach such a course. It seemed like an awful lot of work. I suspect I also put it off because the idea of teaching was a scary prospect! (What an irony! I was frightened about teaching a course about overcoming fear!)

One day as I sat at my desk working away, a strong message came into my head: "Go to the New School for Social Research." I couldn't figure out why this message came into my head. I had never attended the New School. I knew no one there. In fact, I didn't even know where it was. Out of curiosity, I decided to go. I told my secretary I was going to the New School and she asked why. I said, "I don't know!" She looked at me strangely as I proceeded out the door.

I got into a cab that delivered me to the door. I walked into the lobby and asked myself, What should I be doing now? I saw a directory and looked at the various departments listed. My eye stopped on "Human Relations Department." That's where I'm supposed to be going, I thought. My mind reasoned that I was probably "sent" there to sign up for a great workshop that they were offering (I was a workshop addict at the time). The idea of teaching at the New School hadn't occurred to me.

I found the door marked Human Relations Department and walked inside. No one was sitting in the reception area. I looked through the door on my right and saw a woman sitting behind her desk. She called out, "Can I help you?" Without thinking about it, I surprised myself by blurting out, "I'm here to teach a course about overcoming fear." Without my realizing it, I was talking to the head of the department, a wonderful woman named Ruth Van Doren.

She looked at me with amazement in her eyes and finally exclaimed, "I can't believe it! I've been searching high and low for someone to teach a course about fear and haven't been able to find one. And today is my deadline—all catalog descriptions must be in today."

She inquired about my credentials and was pleased with what I told her. She then told me she had to run to catch a bus and asked me quickly to write up a course description. I did. She handed the description to her secretary and ran out the door thanking me profusely.

I stood there in a state of shock! I had no conscious intention of proposing a course that day! And what I had imagined would be an arduous task taking months—preparing and presenting my teaching proposal—took exactly twelve minutes! Had I logically thought it through, I would never have approached the New School to teach a course. I would have gone to my alma maters, Hunter College or Columbia University, where I was known. The New School would not have even entered my logical mind. But it definitely had entered my intuitive mind!

Teaching that course was a turning point in my life. My experience was so positive and felt so right that I decided to leave my job of ten years to become a teacher and a writer of self-help books. It is significant that the name of that first class that I taught was Feel the Fear and Do It Anyway! I often wonder if I had *not* listened to my intuition that fateful day, if the book of the same name or any of my other books (including this one) would ever have been written! From this very powerful experience in my life, I came to understand that *there is something within me that has a bigger plan for my life than I am capable of imagining.*

Remember that our minds, when governed by the Lower Self, aren't capable of imagining the grand possibilities that are there for us. Therefore, it is important that we learn to tune in to a part of us that has much greater vision, the Higher Self.

People ask me how to know if it is their intuition speaking when they are being guided or when it is the Lower Self disguising itself as the Higher Self. That's a good question. My answer is that, in the beginning, we need to play with it a bit. Experiment with little things. If you get an internal message to call so and so, and it makes no sense, call anyway. See what happens. Or go somewhere where you are being "led" to go. Or read a book that seems to jump out at you in the bookstore. And so on.

One clue that it is a message from the Higher Self is that it has a purpose for good. When we know that the action we are being led to take is a positive one, then we know we are probably on the wavelength of the Higher Self.

Another exercise that has been very helpful to me comes from Ram Dass, one of my favorite spiritual teachers. When I know I will be faced with having to make a decision, instead of lamenting, "What should I do?" the more peaceful approach is simply to say, "I wonder what Susan is going to do."

When I say, "I wonder what Susan is going to do," in a sense I become the *observer* rather than the decision maker. I distance myself from the drama. I trust that Susan will be led by the wisdom within her, and I put the issue out of my mind. Later I find myself living into the answer easily and effortlessly.

I find it also helps to place quotes around the house or office to give you a nudge when you forget to let go and trust. Include some quotes with humor such as . . .

"When it starts to rain, let it."
Unknown

"Don't push the river. (It flows by itself.)"
Barry Stevens[4]

"People plan. God laughs!"
Unknown

A little levity in the context of an addiction goes a long way!

Now that you have some of the basics of unsetting your heart, the next two chapters help you integrate this important concept into many areas of your life. Remember, as soon as you leave the Lower Self behind and surrender to the events surrounding your life, you are free to enter the Higher Self where the fear, upset, and disappointment disappear and new opportunities for a beautiful life are *constantly* placed before you.

IS WELL ALL IS WELL ALL IS WELL ALL IS WELL ALL IS WELL ALL IS WELL ALL IS WELL ALL IS WELL ALL
WELL ALL IS WELL ALL IS WELL ALL IS WELL ALL IS WELL ALL IS WELL ALL IS WELL ALL IS WELL ALL IS WELL
IS WELL ALL IS WELL ALL IS WELL ALL IS WELL ALL IS WELL ALL IS WELL ALL IS WELL ALL IS WELL ALL
WELL ALL IS WELL ALL IS WELL ALL IS WELL ALL IS WELL ALL IS WELL ALL IS WELL ALL IS WELL ALL IS WELL
IS WELL ALL IS WELL ALL IS WELL ALL IS WELL ALL IS WELL ALL IS WELL ALL IS WELL ALL IS WELL ALL
WELL ALL IS WE   WELL ALL IS WELL
IS WELL ALL I   ALL IS WELL ALL
WELL ALL IS WE   WELL ALL IS WELL
IS WELL ALL I   ALL IS WELL ALL
WELL ALL IS WE   WELL ALL IS WELL
IS WELL ALL IS WELL ALL IS WELL ALL IS WELL ALL IS WELL ALL IS WELL ALL IS WELL ALL IS WELL ALL
WELL ALL IS WELL ALL IS WELL ALL IS WELL ALL IS WELL ALL IS WELL ALL IS WELL ALL IS WELL ALL IS WELL
IS WELL ALL IS WELL ALL IS WELL ALL IS WELL ALL IS WELL ALL IS WELL ALL IS WELL ALL IS WELL ALL
WELL ALL IS WELL ALL IS WELL ALL IS WELL ALL IS WELL ALL IS WELL ALL IS WELL ALL IS WELL ALL IS WELL
IS WELL ALL IS WELL ALL IS WELL ALL IS WELL ALL IS WELL ALL IS WELL ALL IS WELL ALL IS WELL ALL
WELL ALL IS WELL ALL IS WELL ALL IS WELL ALL IS WELL ALL IS WELL ALL IS WELL ALL IS WELL ALL IS WELL
IS WELL ALL IS WELL ALL IS WELL ALL IS WELL ALL IS WELL ALL IS WELL ALL IS WELL ALL IS WELL ALL
WELL ALL IS WELL ALL IS WELL ALL IS WELL ALL IS WELL ALL IS WELL ALL IS WELL ALL IS WELL ALL IS WELL
IS WELL ALL IS WELL ALL IS WELL ALL IS WELL ALL IS WELL ALL IS WELL ALL IS WELL ALL IS WELL ALL
WELL ALL IS WELL ALL IS WELL ALL IS WELL ALL IS WELL ALL IS WELL ALL IS WELL ALL IS WELL ALL IS WELL
IS WELL ALL IS WELL ALL IS WELL ALL IS WELL ALL IS WELL ALL IS WELL ALL IS WELL ALL IS WELL ALL
WELL ALL IS WELL ALL IS WELL ALL IS WELL ALL IS WELL ALL IS WELL ALL IS WELL ALL IS WELL ALL IS WELL
IS WELL ALL IS WELL ALL IS WELL ALL IS WELL ALL IS WELL ALL IS WELL ALL IS WELL ALL IS WELL ALL
WELL ALL IS WELL ALL IS WELL ALL IS WELL ALL IS WELL ALL IS WELL ALL IS WELL ALL IS WELL ALL IS WELL
IS WELL ALL IS WELL ALL IS WELL ALL IS WELL ALL IS WELL ALL IS WELL ALL IS WELL ALL IS WELL ALL
WELL ALL IS WELL ALL IS WELL ALL IS WELL ALL IS WELL ALL IS WELL ALL IS WELL ALL IS WELL ALL IS WELL
IS WELL ALL IS WELL ALL IS WELL ALL IS WELL ALL IS WELL ALL IS WELL ALL IS WELL ALL IS WELL ALL

7

LET LIFE HAPPEN . . . PERFECTLY

Peace is the vibrant space which stimu-
lates the dance of kindness, merriment,
and freedom.

Unknown

P EACE DOES, INDEED, HELP US DANCE
the dance of kindness, merriment, and freedom. And where does
this elusive peace come from? We've learned that it certainly
doesn't come from the external dramas in our life! No, peace comes
from the place within—the Higher Self. It is here that we learn how
to let go of our addictive demand for life to happen the way we want
it to happen!

Whether we are talking about the little things in life or the
really big things, it is necessary that we stop hanging on to the way it
is "supposed to" be. Make LET GO be your motto whenever upset
enters your life—past, present, and future. Here are some suggestions as to how you can begin to retrain the thinking that keeps you
immersed in struggle.

LET GO OF THE LITTLE THINGS

I am constantly amazed how the little things in life cause us so much
upset and struggle. I have watched many people (including myself!)
ruin a lovely dinner out because the table wasn't right, or the service
was slow, or the lighting was wrong, or the waiter wasn't polite
enough. I'm sure you would agree these are very unimportant inci-
dents in the GRAND SCHEME of life, yet they seem to put people

in a very bad temper and take away all their peace, and the peace of everyone around them!

Yes, our addiction to control affects even the smallest and pettiest events in our lives. Alan Cohen tells us a wonderful story about his great moment of awakening when it came to letting go of such trivial things in his life.[1] This moment didn't come upon him on the top of a great mountain or at the edge of a vast ocean. No, his moment of awakening came to him at McDonald's. (There are many Paths to awakening!)

He reports that from the minute he walked into McDonald's for a quick lunch, he was miserable. He remembered someone telling him there was sugar in the french fries. He imagined the presence of preservatives in the apple pie. He lamented the preponderance of noisy kids stifling the whole environment, and on and on and on. Nothing was right. He vowed he would never return. But, then, as he sat there in what he called "the smog of my own thoughts," the voice from his Higher Self came through loud and clear. It asked him a profound question that made all the difference:

"What if this were all all right?"

He gasped, "What do you mean, all right? This is terrible!" His Higher Self answered:

"What if nothing around you holds any power to make you unhappy?"

What a concept! What a breakthrough! All of a sudden, Alan Cohen saw everything with new eyes. He looked at the boisterous kids and decided their laughter and shouts reflected their joy. What's wrong with a little joy in the middle of the afternoon? He decided a little sugar and preservatives wasn't going to affect his ability to love. He decided that everything that was previously annoying him was totally all right. He said:

"Something happened to me when I let it all be okay. I felt relief. My heart opened. I was at peace. I had found the answer to being there. I had found the answer to all of life. Just let it be."

With this realization, he got in line for some more french fries and apple pie, which he concluded was what they serve in heaven! And he basked in the wonder of letting it all be all right.

This is such a wonderful example of how different our experience of life can be when we listen to the Higher Self instead of the Lower Self. After I read Alan Cohen's story, I thought about all the little things in my life that I was constantly obsessing about—getting the right table in the restaurant, the weather, the stock market, the traffic, points of view that were different from mine, other people's behavior, getting everywhere on time. And so on. What a struggle!

What if any table I got was okay? What if the weather was perfect exactly as it was? What if my money in the stock market was irrelevant to my sense of security? What if the delays in traffic were just part of the scene? What if other people's opinion had nothing to do with my happiness? Or their behavior? What if life would go on joyfully even if I arrived at an appointment a little bit late?

What if *everything* was okay?

What a freedom! Then I would be wearing the world just as a loose garment instead of struggling to make it all different than it is.

As I said earlier, so much of our struggle with life has to do primarily with minor things in life. The big things often pull forward an incredible sense of power and inner knowing. I had breast cancer many years ago, and I handled it beautifully. I made it a triumph instead of a tragedy. By way of contrast, I got a very bad hair perm three weeks before my present marriage. Did I make that a triumph? No way. You would have thought my world was coming to an end. Even after the wedding, I was upset for months until the frizzy hair finally grew out.

Does this make sense on a Spiritual level? Absolutely not! My Higher Self could care less about my hair. It's hard to believe my

Lower Self cared so much, but it did. Had I known what I know today, I would have been in a much better position to say to myself,

Let go. Let peace. Let joy.

So think about the many little things that cause upset in your life. Getting a dent in your new car. Forgetting to buy something at the supermarket. Sitting in the airport for two hours because the plane was delayed. Rain when you have invited people over for a picnic. It's at these times that we really need to take a step back and ask ourselves that profound question: *"What if this were all all right?"*

As I look at the laughing Buddha sitting on my desk, I now understand that one of the reasons he is always laughing is that *he already knows that everything is all right!* I think all of us should paste stickers everywhere we can see them that say, "What if this were all all right?" It would help to remind us to pull ourselves out of the horseradish of our Lower Self and lift us to the freedom of our Higher Self.

As an exercise, write down all the situations in your life that are causing you struggle and ask yourself about each situation: "What if this were all all right?" Each time you ask this question, take a deep breath and relax. You will experience a momentary feeling of peace. Do this over and over again until just the asking of the question is associated with a deep breath and a feeling of relaxation. And as you go through each day, notice where you are trying to control everything around you. Add it to your list and keep asking yourself, "What if this were all all right?"

Another effective way to pull ourselves out of the prison of our Lower Self is simply to *change our focus*. Why do we always look at what's missing instead of what's there? Why do we always look at the bad instead of the good? Why do we always focus on the ugliness instead of the beauty? When we focus on what's missing, or what's bad, or what's ugly, we are operating from the level of the Lower Self. Why not rise above the Lower Self and see what the world looks like from the Higher Self?

For example, what if instead of focusing on the lousy table at the restaurant, we focused on the wonderful company, the luxury of having someone else cook our meal, the abundance of having enough money to pay for the meal, the blessing of good health to be out and about on a beautiful evening, and on and on and on. The table might still be lousy, but 99 percent of the evening is wonderful. Why focus on 1 percent?

We can create this shift in focus in all areas of our life that bring us upset. The truth is that blessings surround us all the time. That shift in focus isn't a delusion. In fact,

We are deluding ourselves when we focus on the bad!

Read that again! So when that lousy table comes up and there are no others available, you say to yourself, "Yes the table may be lousy, but look at all that is wonderful in this situation. How blessed I am!" Indeed, when life is seen in this way, we are a step farther in conquering our control addictions, and there is very little that can take away our peace.

LET GO OF THE BIG THINGS

Letting go sounds reasonable when we are talking about a table in a restaurant. Does the question, "What if this were all all right?" work in terms of the loss of loved ones, bankruptcy, the loss of our home, and all the other crisis situations that can befall any of us at any time? You know my answer to that. YES! We have two choices:

Either we make it all all right or we make ourselves helpless victims.

The former is definitely the preferable choice to make! In order to truly end the struggle and dance with life, it is essential that we learn to let go of the victim mentality. Victims can't enjoy life. They are too busy feeling sorry for themselves, feeling powerless, being martyrs, worrying, complaining, seeing the dark side of life, appreciating nothing, and blaming everyone. Not a happy picture! No evidence of the Higher Self here! And yet we need only look around and notice the growing epidemic of victimization. Charles Sykes points out the ludicrousness of the situation:

> "Victim status is now claimed not only by members of minority groups but increasingly by the middle class, millionaire artists, students at Ivy League colleges, 'adult children,' the obese, co-dependents, victims of 'lookism' (bias against the unattractive), 'ageism,' 'toxic parents,' and the otherwise psychically scarred—all of whom are now engaged in an elaborate game of victim one-upmanship."[2]

Unfortunately, instead of people being taught to take responsibility for their experiences of life, they are being given invitations to abdicate responsibility. Murder, rape, and every means of violence and degradation are being excused because of disadvantaged childhoods or abusive marriages or whatever. Ultimately, this works for no one.

By definition, the victim mentality signals a total loss of power and a miserable life. We have to ask ourselves, "Why are we immersing ourselves in such heaviness and misery? Why are we competing to see who could be the most pathetic? Why do we choose to disempower ourselves in this way?"

We do it because we haven't yet found our way to the Higher Self. As a result we find ourselves drowning in the toxicity of the Lower Self where we feel frightened and ill-equipped, and where we are certainly misinformed! As a result, we cop out of the responsibility for taking charge of our lives. We lose the power that helps us create life the way we want to live it. We become blind to all the possibilities that life's challenges offer us.

To pull ourselves out of this mess, it is necessary to use one of my favorite tools for pulling away from the victim mentality:

PICK UP THE MIRROR INSTEAD OF THE MAGNIFYING GLASS![3]

We do this not to blame ourselves (*any* kind of blame is self-defeating) but to make ourselves strong. By picking up the mirror we learn that we can't blame anyone for walking all over us; we can only notice when we are not getting out of the way. We learn that we—not our society or our parents or anything or anyone out there—are the creators of our own experiences of life. We learn that we are responsible for our *reactions* to whatever life hands us.

Once we understand this important reality, our Journey to the best of who we are—our Higher Self—can begin. As we make that Journey, our heart begins to open, the struggle vanishes, and the dance of life and love begins.

Another one of my favorite tools for pulling out of the victim mentality is . . .

Say YES to your Universe!

As I describe in *Feel the Fear and Do It Anyway*, saying YES to your Universe means *letting go* of resistance and *letting in* the possibilities inherent in any of life's situations. Saying YES is definitely a tool of our Higher Self! Conversely, saying NO is definitely a tool of our Lower Self! In the way I am using it, saying NO means being a victim. It means resisting opportunities for growth. Saying NO creates tension, exhaustion, and struggle. Saying YES reduces upset and anxiety and lets you become the creator of enriching new life experiences. *Saying YES doesn't mean giving up*. It means *getting up* and acting on your belief that you can create meaning and purpose in whatever life hands you. It means moving into the realm of action. Here you are able to . . .

Find the blessing. Find the lesson to be learned. Find the strength you never thought you had. Find the triumph.

Saying YES is a very powerful tool indeed!

As I said earlier, I was diagnosed with breast cancer many years ago. It was then that I learned the profound wisdom in saying YES to the Universe. I am eternally grateful that I was able to tap into the wisdom within that helped me find the blessing, find the lessons to be learned, find the strength I never thought I had—and ultimately to find the triumph.

Because of all the lessons I learned, I can actually say that breast cancer was one of the most empowering experiences of my life. What did I learn? I learned that sexuality has nothing to do with a breast! (Do you hear that, women?) I learned that illness often comes from negative emotions, so I made a concerted effort to deal with all the old anger and pain I was holding. That made a tremendous difference in my life! I learned that a crisis can deepen love—and I married the beautiful man who never left my side. I learned that we can't take life for granted, so we better enjoy it while we have it. I learned all this and more.

Although I received so many blessings from my experience of cancer, I wouldn't consciously choose cancer as my favorite way of learning. (I'd probably choose a vacation in Italy instead!) But *cancer is what life handed me* and, thankfully, I let my Higher Self instead of my Lower Self be my guide. I chose to say YES and opened to all the possibilities instead of saying NO and seeing myself as a helpless victim.

You will find some incredible stories of people saying YES to their Universe in *Feel the Fear and Do It Anyway*, including Victor Frankl's ability to say YES to the horrors of a concentration camp. These stories demonstrate the immense power we have to transcend to the highest level of who we are despite *any* circumstances in our life.

Many of us are victims out of habit. Often we don't even realize what we are doing when we are doing it. I was at a cocktail party recently when someone introduced herself to me as follows: "I'm Laura, an adult child of an alcoholic." I was a bit taken aback. I thought to myself, "How limiting!" Then I thought of all the other labels that people seem to identify with lately. "I am an incest sur-

vivor." "I am a breast cancer survivor." "I am a victim of rape."
Whereas this kind of labeling may be an appropriate introduction in
the context of a self-help or therapist-led group, *it is very inappropriate as a label for living.*

There is danger in defining ourselves by victim labels instead of
by the incredible strength we were given to deal with our circumstances, no matter how ghastly they are. Yes, it is important to deal
with the psychological implications of disadvantaged childhoods
and the like, but . . .

HEALTH DOES NOT COME FROM PERPETUATING SICKNESS!

As I said earlier, I love the fact that there are so many self-help
groups, therapist-led groups, twelve-step programs, and so on that
help people become strong as a result of their past. I encourage people
to attend. I know that the group process has made an incredibly positive difference in my life. At the same time, I warn people to LEAVE
ANY PROGRAM OR GROUP (OR ANY THERAPIST, FOR
THAT MATTER) THAT FEEDS THE VICTIM MENTALITY.[4]

So the next time you have an occasion to define yourself, instead of sending the message I am a victim, send the message I am
the recipient of many blessings. Repeat this to yourself over and
over again as you go through each day. Soon the load of negativity
will lighten, and you will begin to feel free to notice all the beauty in
your life.

I can't think of a way of being in life that is more destructive to
our self-respect and the general quality of our life than seeing ourselves as victims. A wonderful book that takes this concept farther is
Legacy of the Heart by Wayne Muller.[5] Its subtitle is *The Spiritual Advantages of a Painful Childhood.* What a powerful idea—that those of
us with painful childhoods are "advantaged"! We can all draw wonderful things from our experiences—past, present, and future. In
doing so, the victim mentality fades into the distance.

Also, we need to stop others from characterizing us as victims.
For example, when someone learned that I had had breast cancer a

number of years ago, she looked at me with a "poor you" look on her face. "Oh, you're a cancer survivor." This characterization of who I am didn't sit well with me. I said, "No, I'm a very lucky human being, who happened to have had cancer as part of my experience of life. It was an enriching experience that taught me many important lessons. I consider it a gift and I'm grateful to be alive today." She was a bit taken aback in a world where "poor you" is considered a compliment!

In a larger context, we are constantly bombarded with messages from those who are intent on telling us that we are oppressed in some way—physically, emotionally, financially, genderwise, and so on. What this suggests is that we haven't the strength, intelligence, or ability to handle our own lives. It means they see us as helpless, hopeless, and weak. It means they see us as incapable of picking ourselves up, standing tall, and living a life filled with confidence and purpose. How insulting!

The truth is that we are not helpless, hopeless, weak, and incapable. The truth is that we are not powerless! The truth is that *all things in our life can be used to empower us, no matter how difficult they are at the time.* To me life is about bringing forth the best of who we are. When we play the role of victim and habitually blame others, we are not bringing forth the best of who we are. We are making ourselves powerless!

Instead of blaming, we need to learn how to take charge of our lives, honor who we are, and create powerful and beautiful lives for ourselves. We can't do this with anger and blame; we can do it only by drawing on the immense amount of strength that lies within our being.

If there is a hell on earth, living as a victim with feelings of anger and blame defines it. If there is a heaven on earth, living powerfully and lovingly as the creator of our own lives defines it.

Make no mistake. Anytime we blame anyone or anything for what is happening in our lives, we are giving away all our power.

I was invited to a "celebration" created by Wayne Muller for people living with AIDS and their families, friends, and loved ones. More than a thousand people filled the church in which the celebration was held. How do you *celebrate* AIDS? With three hours filled with singing, praying, sharing stories, laughing, lighting candles, and generally enjoying the gift of life.

These were three hours where everyone was saying YES to the Universe, even one that included AIDS. It was evident to all of us that although grief is a natural part of such a devastating illness, so are relationships being healed, hearts being opened, friendships being deepened, and families coming together to become meaningful participants in this world.

Carlo, a dear friend of mine, became afflicted with chronic fatigue syndrome, which kept him virtually homebound for a couple of years. This was difficult for a man who had been very active. Initially, he resisted what was happening and made himself miserable. But after a while, he stopped resisting. He let go. He said YES and decided to use the time to find the blessings.

He learned to meditate. He wrote a book. He, who had been in the helping professions, learned to ask for help and found out what it meant to be on the receiving side. He learned how precious his friends were as they rallied to his side. Most important, he got in touch with his inner power and love. He said to me one day,

> "When all your supports are taken away from you, you find what really supports you."

Carlo discovered the trust that comes from a life lived from the Higher Self. He let go of many of the attachments of his Lower Self, most important, his need to control.

So think of all that could go wrong with your life in a *major* way and decide that it's all all right! Decide that you have the power to say YES to it all. Your saying YES guarantees that you will find the limitless source of inner strength that lies within us all. *There is no greater comfort than that.* When we achieve that state of comfort, we can let go of our need to control even the big things in our lives. We truly understand the wisdom in the popular saying:

Don't sweat the small stuff . . . and it's *all* small stuff!

From the place of the Higher Self, it's all small stuff indeed! What's really BIG is our capacity to take in all that life hands us and use it to access the huge amount of power and love we hold inside.

8

FEEL SAFE IN A
DANGEROUS WORLD

> *For true peace of mind we must acknowledge whatever fault we live upon, whatever time bomb ticks in our closet, and enjoy our Shangri-la nonetheless. It isn't the absence of the problem; it is how one lives in its presence that matters.*
>
> Chungliang Al Huang[1]

I CERTAINLY DON'T NEED TO REMIND you that this is a world where dangers lurk everywhere. Our newspapers and television news shows present us with a daily litany of violence, incurable diseases, natural disasters, and an untold number of tragedies that could befall any one of us, at any age, at any time of day. It makes one want to turn and run the other way. But where is there to run? Nowhere!

Can we train ourselves to let go and dance with life in such an environment of seemingly heightened danger? Again, the answer is YES! Gertrude Stein once said,

"Considering how dangerous everything is, nothing is really very frightening!"

I know she's right! A few years ago a disease was reported in my home state of New Mexico. It's called the Hantavirus, and it killed more than twenty people in the state before doctors discovered what it was and how to treat it. At the time we heard about the disease, my husband and I looked at each other and said, "What are we doing here? Let's leave!" We then started to name other places where we might want to live. "We could move back to Los Angeles," I said. "But there are earthquakes there," he said. "We could move to Florida," I said. "But there are hurricanes there," he said. And on it went. Eventually, the both of us started laughing with the realization that *nothing's safe*, at least not in the traditional ways we look at safety.

With that realization, our fear of the Hantavirus strangely disappeared. Somehow we were overcome with a sense of calm, the sense that we didn't have to go anywhere to be safe since that place didn't exist! We could stay right where we are.

My friend Ken learned this the hard way. He decided to leave the "dangers" of Manhattan to seek safety for his children. He became the minister of a small church in a sleepy little town where he thought they would be safe. One night, he heard a noise in his daughter's room. He got out of bed to investigate and found that an intruder had come in and was trying to strangle her. Had the sounds not awakened him, his daughter would not be alive today. Ken's story makes us realize that . . .

There is no point in trying to escape danger. Danger is— and has always been—a fact of life. There *never* has been a safe time in history, nor a safe place. Part of the package of being human is that we live in a dangerous world.

So how can we be in this world and not drive ourselves crazy with fear? First, we learn how to surrender. We once again let go of our attachment to the world being any different than it is. And again we ask ourselves the question, "What if this were all all right?" We learn that it has to be all right because it's doubtful that it's ever going to be any other way! With this, we lighten up. We laugh at our predicament. We have a good time in spite of the danger. *If something happens, so be it.*

I find this technique of surrender so powerful in many situations in life; for example, when I am flying in a plane. When the occasional turbulence hits, my automatic reflex is a quickening of the heart and a tightening of my muscles—the body's response to fear. Whenever this occurs, I simply say . . .

"Okay, Universe. Take over, please."

This doesn't mean, "Okay, Universe. Don't let anything happen to the plane. Get me safely to my destination." It means,

"Okay, Universe. Take over, please. Whatever happens, so be it. I trust the Grand Design. I trust it is all happening as it is supposed to happen."

I can't tell you what a relief this kind of thinking brings me. After I ask the Universe to take over, my muscles relax and my heart slows down. I have long ago stopped driving myself crazy by trying to hold up the plane. Exhausting! If the plane goes down, it goes down. Nothing I can do about it. With this kind of thinking, I am then free to end the struggle and enjoy the ride.

Recently floods ravaged the American Midwest. I was struck by the words of one woman whose home was destroyed and who was moving her family out with their very meager possessions. She said:

"My daddy had a good philosophy. He said, 'If there is something you can do about it, get off your butt and do something. If you can't do anything about it, don't worry about it!'"

This woman had a very wise daddy!

Californians, particularly those who live in Los Angeles, set a good example. They're a hardy breed, indeed. They are plagued not only by earthquakes but also riots and fires. As I drove down Sunset Boulevard one day, I saw a wonderful billboard with the following words of noted accessories designer Kenneth Cole:

"Earthquakes, riots, and fires . . . Oh, my!"[2]

It's as though Cole were an observer commenting on the events of the day with little attachment to things being any other way. I know an awful lot of Los Angelenos who have this kind of humorous attitude and are not put off by the happenings of their city. To them, it's still the greatest place in the world to be. All the dangers in the city are just part of the passing scene.

They all "protect" themselves as much as they can, but in the end, they know they have very little control of how the earth is moving or how the fires are spreading or how racial tensions are playing themselves out. The only control they have is *their reaction* to whatever is happening around them. And, for the most part, they handle their reactions marvelously well. They know, as Ken's story portrays, that moving to a "safer" place is no guarantee of safety. They believe that if you love living in a place, you should enjoy every moment you are there and stop worrying about all the things that can befall you.

Michael Ventura wrote a wonderful and insightful article about Californians titled "The Earthquake People," in which he suggests that we are all earthquake people.[3] We all live with a clear and present danger of some sort. And we all have to surrender, to let go of our expectation of safety. He tells the story of the late Achaan Chah Subato, a monk from Thailand. People came to him and asked how anyone can be happy in a world of such impermanence where you cannot protect yourself or your loved ones from harm. Achaan Chah Subato held up a glass and said,

"Someone gave me this glass, and I really like this glass. It holds my water admirably and it glistens in the sunlight. I touch it and it rings. One day the wind may blow it off my shelf, or my elbow may knock it from the table. I know this glass is already broken, so I enjoy it incredibly."

Read that last line again. How profound and how freeing! There's nothing to hold on to when we know that our "glass" is already broken and we better enjoy it now. Yes, in time all that we dearly love today will be a thing of the past. In days, years, decades, and centuries to come, the world as we know it today will *definitely* be changed or gone. Don't freak out with this bit of realism. Rather, see the important lesson to be learned.

Why hold on so tight to things that, in the grand scheme of life, can't be held on to?

All things are forever changing. This is the nature of the world. So instead of worrying about what will ultimately come, the alternative is to enjoy every moment that we have. As with all circumstances in our lives—good or bad—there is much to be learned. We need to stop putting off life. We need to live life to the fullest.

All the dangers in our world are like a blessed wake-up call. They tell us to live life NOW—not tomorrow, not when the children grow up, not when we retire—but NOW!

We don't have to live in fear, even though those moments of fear will come up. We don't have to live in self-denial; that's avoiding the multitude of possibilities for a vibrantly wonderful life. When we know that time is limited on this earth, we can learn much more easily to live for today—not in a self-destructive way, but in a way that can lead to a richness of body, mind, and Spirit. This concept is very freeing to me. I have stopped taking things so seriously. I have learned to let go of many things that were once very important to me. And I have certainly begun living more and more in the NOW.

Cowering in fear robs us of life. The antidote to our fear is simply to say,

"Okay, Universe. Take over, please. Take me where you wish. I'll enjoy the ride."

This is taking refuge in the land of the Higher Self and leaving the realm of the Lower Self behind. This is having the trust that no matter what is happening in our lives, it's all happening perfectly. Joan Borysenko talks of "Spiritual optimism,"[4] which is the kind of attitude we all need in a world that moves and shakes, in a world where life is what happens when we make other plans.

If we don't have Spiritual optimism, we sometimes isolate ourselves from the blissful experiences of life. Those who are afraid to fly miss the experience of flying above the clouds. Those who are afraid of walking down the streets of a big city miss the electric energy that only big cities offer us. Those who are afraid of the wilderness miss the enchantment of nature in all its glory. This is such a huge world that it is truly self-denial when we hold ourselves back because we are trying to hold on too tightly to something that is impermanent.

Yes, we *may* be safer climbing into bed and pulling the covers over our head (unless someone climbs in the window and tries to attack us), but what a waste of a life. *Understand I'm not advocating a life of taking excessive risks like walking down dark city streets late at night, or entering the wilderness unprepared, or speeding in a car, or jumping out of a plane, or playing Russian roulette.* I am talking about accepting the everyday gifts that this world has to offer, without worrying that we will be hurt in the process. We will or we won't. But in the meantime, we will be living a wonderful life. So while you are a visitor to this little planet called Earth, take the advice of my role model, Auntie Mame, who once said,

LIVE! LIVE! LIVE!

9

FIND BEAUTY IN
THE LAND OF TEARS

Life is beautiful,
I have it all.
But even in the sunshine,
One has to cry sometimes.

Susan Jeffers[1]

I WANT TO END THIS SECTION OF the book by introducing you to a secret, unexplored place deep within your being. It is a place that exists within us all, and, in order to heal the hurts that lie deep within us, we need to enter it fully. When we emerge, we are surprised to learn that we are much freer to embrace all that is beautiful in this world.

I came upon this secret place quite unexpectedly many years ago in New York City as I was riding in a bus on Central Park West. Traffic was very heavy and we were moving at a snail's pace. As I sat looking out the window, I noticed a group of schoolchildren walking in twos, heading for the park. It was a warm sunny day in May, and the children's giggles and chatter put a smile upon my face. Each child carried a lunch bag filled with little treasures that some caring person had placed there earlier that morning. My mind got lost in thinking back to those special days when I was a child.

My reverie was suddenly shattered when one little boy's lunch bag burst open, spilling all his treasures on the ground. As I watched his anguished gaze fixated on the ruined contents of his bag, I had to turn away. Somewhere deep within me, it hurt too much, and the tears started rolling down my cheeks. I was surprised at the well of emotion this little incident had released in me. My reaction seemed totally inappropriate to the scene that had occurred. What was going on within me?

I realized that this was not the first time I had felt this puzzling depth of emotion over some relatively innocuous scene that I had witnessed. This was not the first time that some situation outside myself had touched that place within that I have come to call *the Land of Tears*. I knew that the deep sadness that I felt had nothing to do with what was happening in my life at the time. In fact, my life was rich with meaningful work and the love of my family and caring friends. No, the sadness was not about my personal story, but something much broader, much more significant than that. Another perplexing part of the puzzle was that not only did sad things touch the Land of Tears, happy things did as well. Just watching a family reunited at the airport left me sobbing. What was *that* all about?

Through much soul searching, I eventually found the answers to my questions. I came to realize that my tears reflected something I had tried very hard to deny—the Universal hardship that we all experience by virtue of the fact that we are human beings. Life is tough! It hurts a lot! By definition, being truly alive implies a lot of pain.

Who has not at times felt rejected, unloved, helpless, lonely, not quite good enough? Who has not cried at the unfairness of so many happenings in their lives? Who has not inwardly prayed that things like death and cancer and nuclear war won't happen to them and theirs? Who has not had to come to terms with the fact that there are times we have to say good-bye to those we love most? Who has not witnessed all the pain, suffering, and destruction that exists in this world? Life is about facing all this and so much more.

But why the tears in the face of great joy? This was not difficult to figure out. Isn't it all part of the same thing? Isn't joy about reaching the other side of struggle? Didn't that family reunited at the airport first have to go through the pain of separation, time of loneliness, and fear of loss before the joy of reunion? Their tears and hugs suggested they did. Whether it's the sorrow of good-bye or the joy of hello, it's all part of the same package. It all signifies the human condition.

The last and most important part of the puzzle was, "Why did I have to turn away?" This was the tough one. I finally realized it was because I couldn't look life squarely in the face. For years, I tried very hard to avoid the Land of Tears. I needed to believe that life should always be happy. To perpetuate this delusion, I became a pseudopositive thinker, one who was in constant denial about the pain of living. I was avoiding an essential element in the art of *genuine* positive thinking. I was avoiding the Land of Tears.

I became such a pseudopositive thinker that I became detached, disconnected from my own pain and disconnected from other people's pain as well. In fact, I dismissed their despair as weakness. They were touching feelings I was desperately trying to disinherit. Hence, I couldn't feel connection and empathy, only disdain.

But trying to uphold the fantasy that this is the best of all possible worlds is a difficult thing for the mind to do in the face of overwhelming evidence to the contrary. Just reading the daily newspaper should cause the slightest bit of doubt. Yet I kept denying all the pain within me and around me. It was as though I was holding my finger in the hole of the proverbial dike, trying to hold back the flood of tears that lived within me. But the dike would leak every once in a while, as it did when I saw the pain on that little boy's face as his lunch spilled all over the ground.

One day the dike cracked open, and I could no longer hold back the flood. I realized that all the hunger, war, greed, illness, unfairness, pain, and horror in the world were real. It was not a figment of anyone's imagination or a result of negative thinking. The despair poured all over me and through me. What a blow to a well-defended personality! It took a while to absorb the shock of my despair and restructure my life in a more genuine and life-affirming way. But it was well worth the effort.

Having made the Land of Tears an integral part of my life so many years ago has had enormous benefits. In the first place, I've joined the human race. When I watch the struggle of others, I can now connect with my own struggle, and we are no longer strangers. I don't have to turn away. I can embrace them and their pain and let them know they are not alone. I'm a lot kinder and more patient, and that makes me feel good. I've learned to judge others a lot less harshly, remembering that deep within them exists their own Land of Tears, no matter how they may appear on the outside. What they do and say is just their way of handling hurt. I actually feel younger then I did way back then. I have much more energy. I feel lighter, freer, more able to dance with life. What a merciful relief not to have to hold back that raging river of emotion any longer!

Now, when the deep sadness comes over me, I can let it be there like a warm blanket. I don't have to push it away. It feels so good to just let the tears flow freely. When I let the tears wash over me, I feel cleansed and healed. And when the river of tears is empty, I am freer to enjoy the delights the world has to offer, without a layer of sadness dampening my joy.

Paradoxically, my letting in the pain of being human has allowed me to embrace the joy of being human. The exquisite moments expand and expand—the moments I am infused with energy and aliveness, the moments I feel connected as part of the human family, the moments I let go of the struggle and feel myself dancing with life. All the pain in the world cannot deny the existence of these exquisite moments.

There are times when I forget about the Land of Tears, times when I am very busy and live my life as though those feelings of sadness about the state of the world aren't there. I find myself avoiding the news or avoiding movies that I know have unhappy endings or avoiding phone calls or visits to elderly relatives who remind me of the difficulties aging presents. But it doesn't take me long to recognize the symptoms of repressed pain, and I allow myself a good healthy cry. Immediately, I am free to face the bad news and attend movies with unhappy endings and bring love and caring to elderly relatives who welcome my presence in their lives. And I thank the Land of Tears for the blessed peace that it brings into my life.

When I presented all of the above in one of my workshops, a student raised an interesting point. She said, "I am a heavy-duty crier. I cry all the time. Yet all the crying in the world doesn't give me the peace you're talking about. In fact, it makes me feel rotten! What's the difference?" I realized then that I had forgotten an important piece of my explanation.

As I discussed briefly in Chapter 7, when situations in our life are painful, we have a choice of saying YES to the pain or NO. The tears that come from either choice are very different indeed.

> The tears of YES come from the understanding that pain is just part of the richness of life.

> The tears of YES come from the understanding that no matter how difficult life gets, you can handle anything that comes your way and emerge from it stronger and wiser.

> The tears of YES reflect the bittersweetness that lies in many of our sorrowful experiences.

> The tears of YES come from the acknowledgment of the human condition and the understanding that we are all in it together.

You can see that the tears of YES come from the Higher Self, the best of who we are. They are cleansing, part of the healthy human process of letting go of pain. The tears of YES allow us to be the creator of our life, not a victim of circumstances. The tears of YES make us feel connected and allow us to move forward in a way that helps to heal our own life and the world around us.

In contrast,

> The tears of NO come from a victim mentality, from those who feel they will never recover from the rough deal life has handed them. And with eyes focused on the darkness, you can be sure that they won't.

The tears of NO come from the question "How could this happen to me?" and from the accompanying feelings of hopelessness, powerlessness, and apathy.

The tears of NO come from our blindness to the possible gifts inherent in any painful experience.

The tears of NO come from our inability to understand the ebb and flow of life; instead we are angered and frightened.

The tears of NO come from the Lower Self. As a result, they serve only to weigh us down. They never resolve the fear and the hurt. The tears of the Lower Self are demoralizing not only to the personality but to society as well. They create a culture of self-appointed victims instead of a culture of winners who emerge triumphant in the face of personal setbacks. I'm sure you know many who cry the tears of NO on a regular basis and yet nothing seems to get resolved in their lives. The drama goes on and on and on.

Hence, if you cry a lot yet find that all the tears in the world aren't making you feel any better relative to some situation in your life, understand that is it because you are crying the tears of NO. In some way, you are feeling helpless and/or a victim of circumstances. You know it is time to find the tools to pull yourself out of the horse-radish of the Lower Self and elevate yourself to the broader vision of the Higher Self where you feel powerful, alive, compassionate, loving, safe, and connected to all living things.[2]

If you never or rarely cry, understand that the release of healthy tears—the tears of YES—is important to one's sense of well-being. Even though our society teaches us that crying is a big no-no, our society is wrong. For example:

We have been taught that real men don't cry. In fact, *real men do cry. Fake men don't cry. Real men are real!* They're not actors pretending to be the strong silent type when deep feelings of pain are yearning to come forward.

We have been taught that to cry is to be weak. In fact, we are finding out that there is strength in healthy tears, for both men and women. There is also peace, flow, energy, compassion, and beauty.

We have been taught that taking the Spiritual path means rising *above* pain. In fact, taking the Spiritual path allows the acceptance of *all that is*. It means embracing the darkness as much as the light. In the darkness, many seeds of greatness have been sown.

We have been taught that positive thinkers don't have pain. In fact, as I mentioned earlier, this is pseudopositive thinking. Just as there are healthy and unhealthy tears, there is also healthy and unhealthy positive thinking. Unhealthy positive thinking is about denial. Healthy positive thinking is that which allows in the tears, knowing we will always get to the other side of the pain.

We have been taught that when everything's going great, we are ungrateful if we have feelings of pain. In fact, we are multifaceted human beings involved not only with our own lives but also with the whole human family. Feelings of pain for our world are natural and healthy. How can we have any sense of humanity with a heart of stone that looks away from the sorrow that is an integral part of the human condition?

We have been taught that if we grieve for the suffering and the pain around us, we are not putting our trust in God. In fact, it is through the pain of YES that we become caring human beings as God would have us, instead of what George Bernard Shaw called "feverish, selfish little clods of ailments and grievances complaining that the world will not devote itself to making us happy."[3] Perhaps God is pleading with us not to turn away from the pain around us so that our planet can be healed.

We have been taught that if there is suffering, it is up to us to fix it. In fact, we can't fix it all. But we can stand where we are, make a circle, see what needs to be done, and do it—and trust that there will be others doing the same thing in their little parts of the world.

We have been taught that if we allow in the pain, we will be imprisoned by it. In fact, if we let in the healthy tears of the Higher Self, we will be released. It is the tears of the Lower Self that keep us mired in self-pity and hopelessness.

Given all the erroneous teachings of a Society that is lacking in understanding about the difference between the tears of YES and the tears of NO, it is time to start questioning our upbringing on all levels by asking ourselves, "Does this teaching help me be more loving toward myself and others?" Certainly, hiding our pain from ourselves is not a way of loving ourselves. And because it doesn't allow us to have compassion for others, it's not a way of loving others either.

The need to hide our pain makes us recoil from the tragedy of others; for example, when we find it impossible to telephone others when something terrible happens in their lives. Our excuse is that we don't know what to say, when a simple, "My thoughts are with you," would mean so much. Now we know the truth. The truth is we are afraid that if we let others' pain into our hearts, our own pain will be unleashed as well. When we allow our own tears of YES to flow freely, we automatically come forward to offer comfort to those who are experiencing sorrowful times.

So understand that if tears do not come easily, it's not that the tears aren't there. It's because they are being repressed in some way, either because we were taught that crying is bad and/or because we don't want to face the depth of our own pain. Some of the signs of unshed tears are . . .

Anger, depression, apathy, indifference, fatigue, boredom, avoidance of unhappy realities in life, pseudopositive thinking, guilt, shame, an excessive need to be busy, negativity, fear, substance abuse, an underlying sadness even when things seem to be going well.

All of the above is a form of "psychological numbing."[4] A poignant way of understanding psychological numbing is to see what we do in wartime situations. We create "the enemy." We can't drop bombs on human beings; but we can drop bombs on the enemy. We have to numb ourselves to the fact that we are killing real human beings who hurt and who want to live and love, just as we do.

Psychological numbing creates apathy. It's not that we don't care. It's that we can't face the pain of caring. When we turn away from the homeless, or the aged, or the handicapped, for example, we are turning away from our own pain, our own fear. We all do this to some extent. But we have to understand that there is room in our lives for both the pain and the joy. In fact, *without acknowledging the pain, there can be no joy.*

I'm sure if you look into your own life and the lives of others around you, you will find many other escape routes. But paradoxically, you are escaping nothing. The damage to our lives when we don't allow ourselves to be whole and authentic is evident everywhere we turn—in our relationships, our careers, and our health. It seems as though the more we try to avoid suffering, the more we suffer. When we enter the Land of Tears and unlock the river of emotion that lies within, we experience a catharsis—a cleansing purification and release. It is easy to understand why we have so much energy after a good healthy cry.

Chungliang Al Huang tells of a wonderful Chinese ritual that takes place at funerals. Professional "criers" are hired to help mourners fully express their grief. They yell, scream regrets and other emotions associated with the person who has died, and they encourage everyone to join in. By the time the ceremony is over, the well of tears is dry, and everyone feels freer and at peace.[5]

I talked earlier about simplifying, letting go of the excess baggage in our lives. Unresolved sorrow is one of the biggest pieces of baggage we can carry around with us day in and day out. Carrying this huge river of tears within us with no release obviously prevents us from moving forward in life, prevents us from being the best that we can be, and keeps us exhausted and out of touch with what is truly important in our lives.

We have to understand that life is the coexistence of all opposites, including joy and sorrow. These opposites are meant to flow together, the one embracing the other. Just as there is the male and female within all of us, so there is the light and dark, strong and weak, happy and sad. We don't have to resist these opposites. Just as we can flow in the peace of happy experiences, we can flow in the pain of unhappy experiences. It is the *resistance* that makes life seem unbearable. If we allow ourselves to go with the feelings our body, mind, and Soul are aching to feel, then we are in harmony once again, dancing with life.

Now that you understand the importance of entering the Land of Tears, let me give you some exercises that will induce healing tears when none seem to come.

1. Very often when reading a novel or an article in the newspaper or hearing a story on television, we are moved to tears, either tears of sadness or tears of joy. We then quickly wipe the tears away and go on with our lives. The next time this happens, let yourself be with the tears of sadness or joy and ask yourself what was touched inside of you that created this strong well of emotion.

   Do the same thing when you have seen a movie that opens the door to the Land of Tears. Usually we cry a few tears at the end of a movie and then go out into the sunshine leaving the feelings behind. The next time this happens, carry your tears to the car and let yourself bawl and bawl and bawl. After seeing the movie *Schlindler's List*, I cried in the car for at least a half hour before I turned the engine on to return home. When I finished crying, I felt enriched, more aware, more reflective of how I could use the lessons learned from the movie in my own life. It goes without saying that it is wonderful to explore these emotions with children, who are often moved to tears when watching a film. Even cartoons often bring up strong feelings in both children and adults! Use them to help you find your way to the Land of Tears.

2. Along the same lines, use situations in your life that automatically bring up sadness to jump into the Land of Tears. When my stepchildren left this summer to go back to college, my husband, Mark, said he didn't know what to do with the tears that were lying right beneath the surface. He decided the best thing to do was to get very busy with his work so he didn't have to think about missing his children. I suggested that he instead focus on his sadness and let his tears come up. I also suggested that he write them each a letter expressing his deep feeling of love for them and thanking them for all the joy they bring to his life—the kind of letter few children ever receive from their fathers. He did as I suggested, and when he emerged from his office, he told me of the deep feeling of release and lightness he felt where before there had been only heaviness.

3. After you do the above exercises a number of times, you will be ready for this more advanced exercise that therapist, author, and friend Wayne Muller taught me. I have used it on several occasions and find it very magical in its results.

   a. Start with a book of stories that tugs at the heartstrings. At Wayne's suggestion, I used Stephen Levine's *Meetings at the Edge: Dialogues with the Grieving and the Dying, the Healing and the Healed*.[6] It was a wonderful choice, since it is a book that helps us take a look at death, the one area of our lives that we often go to great lengths to avoid. My answer to that, of course, is to FEEL THE FEAR AND READ IT ANY-WAY!

b. The next step is to find a quiet place in your home or elsewhere where you can be alone. Turning off the phone adds to your sense of privacy.

c. Read just one chapter at a sitting, and as you read, jump into the pain and the beauty of the stories that are presented. Don't suppress any tears that come up. As you start to cry for the pain of those portrayed in the book, you may find tears coming up for pain in your own life as well. Don't suppress these tears either. You may find yourself crying tears that were never shed over your family, friends, a divorce, or death of a loved one.

Once, when doing this exercise, I got in touch with some very deep feelings of pain and guilt for any hurt I might have caused my children when they were growing up. As the tears were released, I closed my eyes, saw my grown children in my mind's eye, and told them how sorry I was for any pain I caused them. This wasn't done as a way of beating myself up. It was just facing the pain of any mistakes I might have made. I understood that I did the best I could given who I was as a young mother, but that doesn't erase the pain of any hurt I may have caused. I cried and cried until there were no tears left, at which point I breathed a sigh of relief, lightness, and peace. I also felt a heightened sense of love and tenderness for my children.

d. Each day, read a new chapter and repeat the above process until you have gone through the entire book. If your experience is anything like mine, by the time you finish the book, you will feel truly lighter, brighter, clearer, and more joyful than you did when you began this exercise. Even more significantly, it will be easier for you to look death squarely in the eye without flinching or turning away. I suspect that so many of our fears in life come from a fear of facing death.

NOTE: *If you feel you are not strong enough to do this exercise right now, trust your intuition.* Wait until you are ready. *Of course, if you are seeing a therapist, consult with him or her to see if this would be an appropriate exercise for you to do at the present time.*

4. One of the most effective ways of learning how to enter the Land of Tears is to join a group. A healthy group, one that does not allow us to feed the "victim" mentality, allows us to see how we can grow from all of our experiences. It also reveals to us that we are not alone in our feelings of pain. And, as others reveal their own pain, it makes it much easier for us to release our own. If you resist opening up to other people, this is a perfect vehicle for you. As you will see, groups offer a safe place to explore the heights and the depths of who we are. So FEEL THE FEAR AND JOIN A GROUP ANYWAY!

5. Another wonderful tool to help us enter the Land of Tears is music. Music is evocative of moments of happiness and sadness in our lives. Think of various pieces of music that pull your heartstrings and use them to induce tears. Once again, ask what those tears are all about and what you can learn about yourself as a result of your reaction to certain pieces of music. Some of us are deeply moved by classical pieces, while others are deeply moved by pop music, or jazz, or scores of various films or shows.

Every time I hear "Somewhere Out There,"[7] I am touched in a very deep place. This song helps me get in touch with the loss of my parents. Even though they died many years ago, there are times I miss them. As I let these tears flow, I can feel the pain of my loss coupled with an appreciation of how lucky I was to have had them in my life. Here is a good example of the bitter-sweet. So find some music that touches you deeply and use it to explore the depths of your being.

6. Take the time to volunteer a couple of hours a week at a home for the aged, or a hospice, or a home for the hand-icapped. Pick the place you *least* want to go. It is a sign that it represents something you are having a hard time looking at. A friend of mine was terrified at the prospect of dying. To help him push through his fear, he began working with people who are terminally ill. He has learned that many of the people he worked with experi-ence, through the process of dying, a closing, a healing, a peace and beauty in their lives that they never felt be-fore. As a result, my friend no longer fears death. *So walk toward the pain; don't run away. Remember that you will al-ways find beauty in the Land of Tears.*

7. If you find you are not able to pull up painful feelings on your own, and you know they are creating a deadening effect on your experience of this world, by all means seek professional help. You want a therapist who encourages you to express your feelings, no matter how irrational they may seem, not one who tells you that your life is good and you have nothing to feel sad about (as one therapist once told me).

So be mindful of the professional help you seek. Some therapists are magical in their ability to guide us to the other side of pain. They know that pain is nothing to be "fixed quick"; it is to be experienced. Ideally, a thera-pist is there as a compassionate companion who can guide you through your pain. Those who try to keep you from feeling your pain usually can't face their own. Remember, therapists are human, too!

8. Use the negativity of the news to test your level of psychological numbness. I hear people saying, "I don't listen to the news anymore. It's far too depressing." At least that's a sign that the horror is getting through! What is more disturbing is that so many of us watch the news with eyes glazed over as bloodied bodies and other horrors march before our eyes. We experience no more emotion toward these events than we do for the commercials that break up the horror! This is a sign that we need to wake up and take notice of what is happening in our world. Our tears help us wake up.

These are just a few ways we can begin to heal the pain and sadness in our lives. I've often been asked,

"Why *is* there so much suffering in the world?"

If this question weighs heavily on your mind, I suggest you stop driving yourself crazy by expecting an answer that we ordinary mortals can't provide. Instead, when the questions comes up, tell yourself the following, which will help to ease any upset you may be feeling:

"I can't see the Grand Design, the Divine plan for this Universe. Therefore, I no longer will ask why. Instead, I will learn to be more trusting. Life includes suffering. And it is up to me to find a way to be more peaceful and compassionate in the midst of the suffering."

One way we all can find that peace and compassion in the midst of the suffering is to enter the Land of Tears with a big YES! in our hearts. When we do this, we are amazed to discover a treasure trove of other riches as well . . .

We learn, we grow, we feel, we care, we share, we love, we heal, we hear, we caress, we touch, we reach out, we

embrace, we unite, we acknowledge, we act, we experience, we open our hearts, we lighten, we understand, we commit, we expand our vision, we become involved, we become wiser, we become freer, we become joyful like the laughing Buddha.

The Land of Tears . . . how sweet it is!

PART III

EMBRACING

THE REWARDS REAP THE REWARDS REAP THE REWARDS REAP THE REWARDS REAP THE REWARDS
THE REWARDS REAP THE REWARDS REAP THE REWARDS REAP THE REWARDS REAP THE REWARDS
THE REWARDS REAP THE REWARDS REAP THE REWARDS REAP THE REWARDS REAP THE REWARDS
THE REWARDS REAP THE REWARDS REAP THE REWARDS REAP THE REWARDS REAP THE REWARDS
THE REWARDS REAP THE REWARDS REAP THE REWARDS REAP THE REWARDS REAP THE REWARDS
THE REWAR   AP THE REWARDS
THE REWAR   AP THE REWARDS
THE REWAR   AP THE REWARDS
THE REWAR   AP THE REWARDS
THE REWAR   AP THE REWARDS

10

FOCUS ON THE RICHES

THE REWARDS REAP THE REWARDS REAP THE REWARDS REAP THE REWARDS REAP THE REWARDS
THE REWARDS REAP THE REWARDS REAP THE REWARDS REAP THE REWARDS REAP THE REWARDS
THE REWARDS REAP THE REWARDS REAP THE REWARDS REAP THE REWARDS REAP THE REWARDS
THE REWARDS REAP THE REWARDS REAP THE REWARDS REAP THE REWARDS REAP THE REWARDS
THE REWARDS REAP THE REWARDS REAP THE REWARDS REAP THE REWARDS REAP THE REWARDS
THE REWARDS REAP THE REWARDS REAP THE REWARDS REAP THE REWARDS REAP THE REWARDS
THE REWARDS REAP THE REWARDS REAP THE REWARDS REAP THE REWARDS REAP THE REWARDS
THE REWARDS REAP THE REWARDS REAP THE REWARDS REAP THE REWARDS REAP THE REWARDS
THE REWARDS REAP THE REWARDS REAP THE REWARDS REAP THE REWARDS REAP THE REWARDS
THE REWARDS REAP THE REWARDS REAP THE REWARDS REAP THE REWARDS REAP THE REWARDS
THE REWARDS REAP THE REWARDS REAP THE REWARDS REAP THE REWARDS REAP THE REWARDS
THE REWARDS REAP THE REWARDS REAP THE REWARDS REAP THE REWARDS REAP THE REWARDS
THE REWARDS REAP THE REWARDS REAP THE REWARDS REAP THE REWARDS REAP THE REWARDS
THE REWARDS REAP THE REWARDS REAP THE REWARDS REAP THE REWARDS REAP THE REWARDS
THE REWARDS REAP THE REWARDS REAP THE REWARDS REAP THE REWARDS REAP THE REWARDS
THE REWARDS REAP THE REWARDS REAP THE REWARDS REAP THE REWARDS REAP THE REWARDS
THE REWARDS REAP THE REWARDS REAP THE REWARDS REAP THE REWARDS REAP THE REWARDS
THE REWARDS REAP THE REWARDS REAP THE REWARDS REAP THE REWARDS REAP THE REWARDS
THE REWARDS REAP THE REWARDS REAP THE REWARDS REAP THE REWARDS REAP THE REWARDS

In the world to come each of us will be called to account for all the good things God put on this earth which we refused to enjoy.

Talmud

HEN I READ THE ABOVE QUOTE for the first time, I gasped. First, I felt ashamed because I knew that over the course of my lifetime I had been given so much . . . and had appreciated so little. Then I felt elated. At last I had been given "permission" to enjoy. More than permission. I was being told that *if I didn't enjoy, there would be consequences to pay!* What a gift!

I then began *consciously* to look around and notice all the good things God put on earth that I refused to enjoy. I was shocked that I had never noticed these things before, except in a very superficial way. I had only glanced at things I should have embraced. Like most of us, I had an immense capacity for taking things for granted! Since then I have learned that,

Taking things for granted is one of the greatest assaults on the quality of our lives.

When we take things for granted, we never get to see the magnitude of the gifts that are constantly being placed before us. As a result, we feel only scarcity instead of abundance.

It's at this point you may be asking, "What are you talking about, Susan? Just look around. The world is a mess!" Yes, the world is a mess. Your life might be a mess. And despite that fact, there is so much to be grateful for that it staggers the imagination.

The riches of the world envelop us, yet we cannot see.

And why can't we see? We can't see because we humans are creatures of habit. And the present habit of our society is to focus on what is terrible about life and ignore what is wonderful. Our task, then, seems very simple—to *stop* focusing on what is terrible in life and *begin* focusing on what is wonderful. But we all know that this task isn't simple at all. In fact, it turns out to be one of our biggest challenges! The reason for this is that old habits are extremely hard to break. Yet in order to truly dance with life, break them we must!

Each of the following chapters contains concepts and tools to help you stop the habit of focusing on what is terrible and begin focusing on what is wonderful. You will see that focusing on what is wonderful can be achieved in many different and delightful ways. As you read, remember that . . .

In order to break any habit, repetition of the preferred behavior is a must!

Without it, you will keep falling back into old patterns. Repetition allows you, little by little, to shift your awareness to the sumptuous banquet that has been set before you. And you will wonder why previously you weren't able to see what is so obvious now.

It was a wise person who said, "Life is a banquet and most poor bastards are starving to death!" As you open your eyes and really SEE, you will starve no more. You will learn that . . .

Your joy, your happiness, your satisfaction, and your ability to dance with life depend solely on what you pay attention to.

Thankfully, what you pay attention to is entirely up to you!

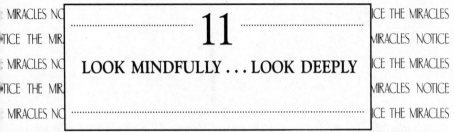

11

LOOK MINDFULLY . . . LOOK DEEPLY

Magical power, marvelous action!
Chopping wood, carrying water.

A Chinese Zen master

THE ZEN MASTER WHO GAVE US the above quote over a thousand years ago was very wise indeed. But, as you can see from the following passage, he was no wiser than Winnie the Pooh, a very lovable bear and one of my favorite story-book characters.

> "When you wake up in the morning, Pooh," said Piglet at last, "What's the first thing you say to yourself?"
>
> "What's for breakfast?" said Pooh. "What do you say, Piglet?"
>
> "I say, 'I wonder what's going to happen exciting today?'" said Piglet.
>
> Pooh nodded thoughtfully. "It's the same thing," he said.[1]

What Winnie the Pooh and our Zen master both tell us is that we can embrace the gifts of magic and excitement in the most ordinary of events—chopping wood, carrying water, eating breakfast, balancing our checkbook, getting our car washed, driving to work, caring for a loved one, working, brushing our teeth, and so on. The trick is to learn how to live in the moment, paying attention to the wonder of it all.

For us in Western society, this idea of living in the moment is very foreign. As I pointed out in Chapter 3, most of us are caught in the trap of *preparing* to live instead of living NOW.

When I go to college . . . then. When I graduate . . . then. When I get married . . . then. When I have kids . . . then. When the kids go off on their own . . . then. When I go on vacation . . . then. When I get a new job . . . then. When I get a divorce. . . then. When I make enough money. . . then. When I retire . . . then.

"When . . . then" seems to govern our lives. I was struck by the message Rabbi Zalman Schachter-Shalomi gave to an audience of elderly people. He told them that aging was their time for harvesting, for reaping the rewards. He said, "We have already plowed, sown seed, but we haven't yet harvested."[2]

Although I certainly applaud his message that aging is a time of harvesting instead of a time of deterioration, I believe that . . .

We don't have to wait until we are old to gather the riches; we can gather them every day of our lives.

While all ages are the "right time" for harvesting, we have to get past the conditioning of our when . . . then society that has taught us to plow, sow the seeds, wait, and (maybe) reap later. And it helps to get past our unfortunate conditioning by recognizing how fraught with errors it is. For example, it's a pity to waste so much of our life waiting. Our faulty conditioning has led us to believe that the enjoyment is supposed to come only *after* all the work has been done, which seems to be never! Wouldn't it make more sense to begin enjoying NOW, *while* all the work is being done? It is Ralph Waldo Emerson who said,

> "Tomorrow will be like today. Life wastes itself whilst we are preparing to live."

How depressing! It makes sense to end this wasteful habit of "preparing" to live and begin living NOW!

Also harvesting is a learned skill. This means that if we don't learn how to do it when we are young, how will we know how to do it when we are old? It is a fact that many people retire, hoping *finally* to reap the rewards of all their hard work. But they haven't a clue as to how to do this and often go into a deep depression. Some die shortly thereafter, and others actually commit suicide. They simply have never learned how to harvest their lives.

On the brighter side, there are those who love retirement. They truly enjoy the riches that aging has to offer. And if you looked into their past, you would probably find that they enjoyed the riches before retirement as well. They had learned the art of harvesting *before* aging came upon them.

So let me show you some of the basic principles of harvesting, of adopting the attitude of Winnie the Pooh and our Chinese Zen master who reaped the beauty and excitement of life in even the most ordinary of everyday events.

LOOK MINDFULLY

I was introduced to the practice of MINDFULNESS many years ago at Esalen Institute where I was attending a week-long workshop focused on the joys of everyday living.[3] One of our assignments was to help cook dinner for the 150 participants there that week. My first thought was, "I didn't come all this way to cook dinner for one hundred and fifty people! I hate to cook!" Thankfully, I went along with the program and was introduced to the concept of mindfulness for the first time.

The kitchen was run by a very Spiritual man who approached his task of cooking with a great deal of attention to the moment and to the wonder of all things. Before we even began to cook, he told us to close our eyes and meditate for a few moments on the great privilege with which we were now being honored—to be able to provide nourishment and enjoyment to other people. This, in itself, put a whole new focus on our "task." *It was no longer a chore, but an honor!*

Next, we were instructed to notice and embrace the blessings that the kitchen provided, such as the sunlight that streamed in through the windows, the beautiful music that was playing, and the appliances that made our task easier. After a few moments of really paying attention to these many blessings, we were all assigned a specific job and told to see ourselves as an important part of the whole. How we did our job would make a difference to everyone around us and to those we would ultimately serve.

We were to cook in silence. And as we cut the bread, or steamed the rice, or sautéed the vegetables, or mixed the ingredients for dessert, we were to be aware of the texture of the food, the colors, the smells—and the ultimate Source of it all. As we worked in quiet unison, our instructor periodically reminded us to focus on the beauty of the moment.

I was amazed to notice that by focusing my attention on the beauty of the NOW, each moment became exquisite. I was filled with a sense of gratitude. I was able to transform a task I hated into one that was nothing short of sublime. I discovered that by focusing on the beauty of the moment, I was able to harvest WHILE I was "plowing and planting the seeds!" The beauty of the process of cooking and serving the meal became my reward. *I didn't have to wait until later to enjoy.*

I remember with intense clarity the cooking of this very special meal even though it happened more than twenty years ago. For me, the experience was mind-altering. I learned that if we look mindfully in this way at all that we do, the world becomes awesomely abundant, and moments of boredom are instantly transformed into exquisite moments.

Now I know you may be thinking to yourself, "It's one thing to cook in such a special environment. But what about those of us who run home from work and breathlessly try to prepare something that's edible for a family that's less than appreciative on a budget that's less than abundant. Surely that's another matter." But is it?

The ritual of purpose, gratitude, focus, and fulfillment that I experienced at Esalen took no more time than a meal prepared with frenzy, frustration, resentment, and/or anger. The food doesn't have to be expensive; it can be simple and healthful as was the meal we cooked that day for 150 people. And the *process* of cooking it was so enjoyable that it didn't much matter to us what reception the food got! We knew we were cooking with a sense of caring and love. It is this sense of caring and love that brings the joy. An appreciative audience is simply the icing on the cake, so to speak; it isn't the essence. I also suspect that with such a positive energy in the preparation of the food, it is bound to get a much more positive reaction than a meal prepared with frenzy, frustration, resentment, and/or anger.

Another benefit of this kind of mindfulness is that for that brief moment in time, we are not focused on the problems we had all day; we are not focused on the fears of tomorrow. We are brought into the present moment. It is living in the NOW. And you may be surprised to learn that . . .

NOW is the only time we have!

The fulfillment of living comes only from being connected in the present moment. And that's what this simple new awareness allows us to create in our lives.

At first glance it seems silly putting full attention on a task such as cooking. But that's precisely the point. *When we are mindful, a task such as cooking (and all our everyday chores) becomes part of the harvest, part of the exquisiteness of life, instead of the boredom of life.* I don't think that's silly; I think it is the height of wisdom!

On the contrary, when we are living a when . . . then kind of life, so many of the common chores of everyday life seem like drudgery as we wait for our two-week vacation. What a waste of a life! As we learn the principles of mindfulness, we can turn those moments of seeming drudgery into moments of pure delight. We don't have to wait for that vacation to enjoy ourselves. We can enjoy ourselves NOW!

I suggest that the next time you find yourself preparing a meal, or cleaning the house, or working at your job outside the home, or driving your car, or gardening, or taking care of an elderly relative, or performing *any* task, you focus on the possibility of that moment bringing you intense joy and satisfaction. Stop the chatter in your mind from telling you that this is a thankless obligation you must do in order to get on with your life. THIS IS YOUR LIFE!

If you see your tasks in life as drudgery, then they are drudgery. On the other hand, if you see them as a gift of the Universe manifest through you, then your tasks in life create a heaven on earth.

What this kind of thinking requires is that we step out of our ordinary frame of reference to see things anew, to make the ordinary in our life extraordinary. As we embrace the ordinary, our lives take on a whole new meaning. Externally, things may remain the same, but internally, a gentle revolution is taking place. Little by little, we begin to replace the struggle in our lives with a sense of abundant flow. And the dance of life has begun.

As you attempt to become a person who lives in the NOW, you will find that it sounds much easier than it really is. As I said earlier, habits are hard to break. Years of living in the past or future have to be overcome. In fact, learning the art of mindfulness is a lifelong process. So don't become discouraged when you keep forgetting. Simply find a way to remind yourself once again.

Remember that each moment of living in the NOW is a step in the right direction. It is all part of your Spiritual path. And as enjoyment increases in your life as a result of living in the NOW, you'll find it easier and easier to remember to look for the blessings right before your eyes.

I suggest that you try giving full attention to something for a few moments of each day, whether it's taking a walk, doing a "chore," or talking to a friend. You'll discover how easily your mind wanders off, but the more you are able to train yourself really to see the opportunity inherent in all that is before you, the more exquisite your life will become.

I've given you just a brief introduction to the concept of mindfulness. I ask you to look into this remarkable Path of fulfillment in greater detail. It is a Path well worth taking.

LOOK DEEPLY

Looking deeply is an extension of looking mindfully. Most of us only skim the surface when we look at what life gives to us. This is why we habitually take things for granted and miss the miracle of it all. For example, there was a time in my life when I used to walk into a supermarket and be bored out of my mind. I'm sure many of you understand exactly what I am talking about! Marketing was a horrible chore I *had to do* before I could get to something I *wanted to do*.

By learning to look deeply, I was able to transform my moments of boredom in the supermarket into many exquisite moments. You might be wondering, How can one have exquisite moments at the supermarket? Let me show you how.

As you walk through the door, just survey the rich array of goodies from which you can choose. Trust me when I tell you that there are few countries in the world that have such abundance.

Then, as you fill your basket with a dozen eggs, a loaf of bread, salad fixings, and a whole basketful of other goodies, look more deeply and notice the huge variety you have to choose from—so many kinds of bread, so many kinds of greens, so many kinds of cereal, so many kinds of dessert. The richness of it all.

As you focus on the abundance in your basket, look a little more deeply and focus on the money you have to pay for your purchases. Even if you can't buy everything you want, you can buy enough to sustain you. (Given the number of overweight people in our society, most of us buy more than enough to sustain us!)

Next, look even more deeply as you focus on the farmers who grew the greens that gave you your salad fixings and raised the chickens that gave you the eggs and grew the grains that gave you the bread and cereal. Focus on the bakers who baked the bread. Focus on the drivers of the trucks, captains of the ships, and pilots of the planes that transported all the riches to your doorstep.

Then look even more deeply as you focus on the staff that is there to serve you. Some of them have been up since very early in the morning to set up the displays in a way to please you. Focus on the people who took a risk and invested their money to create a market to provide you with such sumptuous fare. Focus on the people who built the building that houses the market.

Then look even more deeply and focus on those who created the roads that allowed you to drive your car to this place of wonder and those who manufactured the car that gave you so much mobility.

Then look as deeply as you possibly can and focus on the ultimate Source of it all—God, the Force, the Universal Light, whatever it is for you that created the air, the sun, the water, the earth that makes all growth possible. One can't deny the miraculous rhythm and flow to it all.

We could be there all day and couldn't look deeply enough to encompass the miracle of it all! When you look at the supermarket in this way, it is a monumentally large gift that we have been given. Now can you see how moments of boredom even in the supermarket can be turned into exquisite moments? A dear friend once gave me the following poem by Emily Dickinson, which says it all:

> *As if I asked a common alms*
> *And in my wandering hand,*
> *A stranger pressed a Kingdom*
> *And, I, bewildered, stand.*

We went to the market for a tomato, and when we looked deeply "a stranger pressed a Kingdom" in our hand.

You can begin looking deeply at everything you do in your everyday life—driving your car, working at your office, taking a vacation, reading a book, watching television, gardening, cleaning your house, caring for loved ones. As we look deeply, we see that *in everything we do, we have been handed the Kingdom*. May we always remember this.

I recently saw what I considered a magnificent Vietnamese movie entitled *The Scent of Green Papaya*. For those of us who love action-packed movies, it may be a disappointment. But for those of us who are trying to live mindfully and deeply, it is a riveting movie. The story was about a child who was brought into a Vietnamese home as a servant. This can be a depressing premise for a movie. But the movie was not depressing; it was awe-inspiring.

We watched our little heroine grow up and approach her life with wonder as she looked mindfully and deeply at the magnificence in her everyday world. Her face reflected the marvels she found watching the ants busily going about their work, the frogs jumping here and there, the flowers blossoming in all their glory. We watched the ecstasy on her face every time she cut the green papaya, inhaled its heavenly scent, and felt the texture of all that it contained. And one could feel her sense of privilege as she attended to the needs of those she served, even at those times when her efforts were not appreciated. *As the movie progressed, one didn't feel sorry for her, one envied her appreciation of life*. Were we all to harvest the gifts that our little Vietnamese heroine was able to harvest, *despite her situation in life*, how lucky we would be!

Let me end this chapter with the impassioned plea of Chogyam Trungpa:

"Look. This is your world! You can't not look. There is no other world. This is your world; it is your feast. You inherited this; you inherited these eyeballs; you inherited this world of color. Look at the greatness of the whole thing.

Look! Don't hesitate—look! Open your eyes, don't blink, and look, look—look further."[4]

Hear his plea. Don't miss out on another moment of greatness in your life. Despite what you are doing, your world is rich. *Harvest the riches NOW!*

12

WAKE UP TO THE ABUNDANCE

IT'S AMAZING HOW MANY THINGS we get backward in our thinking! Brother David Steindl-Rast reminds us that no matter how many goodies are lavished upon us in life, unless we are grateful for them, we are still beggars at heart. Not a good feeling! On the other hand, if we notice all the wonderful gifts that are put before us, we feel rich. Even a person who has a difficult life and very little money will be happy if he or she has mastered the art of gratitude.

I used to work with the poor in New York City. I was always amazed at the gratefulness in the hearts of so many who, in a material sense, had very little. What were they grateful for? They were grateful to be alive, to have food on their table, to enjoy the sun on a beautiful day, to have their health, their friends, their family, and to be a contributing force in their community.

At the same time, I was often in the company of people who had a great deal of money. I was always amazed at the *lack* of gratefulness in the hearts of so many. If you were to ask me which of the two were happier, without hesitation I would say the poor with gratefulness in their hearts. *Gratitude creates happiness, not money!*

I remember my mom, just months before she died, sitting with me in her living room on a cold, dreary winter day. She was feeling very weak and in much pain from her tired bones. At one point, when I was in pain about her pain, she looked at me and said, "It's cold outside. . . . I'm warm and cozy inside. My daughter is here . . . sometimes you get lucky." Wow! I was focusing on her pain. She was focusing on her blessings. Thanks, Mom, for that beautiful lesson. What I am talking about here is *very simple*:

When we focus on abundance, our life feels abundant; when we focus on lack, our life feels lacking. It is simply a matter of focus.

As I pointed out in Chapter 9, we can't be in denial about the pain in our life. And just as important,

WE CANNOT BE IN DENIAL ABOUT THE ABUNDANCE IN OUR LIFE!

This is a nation of people totally immersed in denial about the abundance in their lives. We have become a nation of victims, and it's hard for victims to be happy. Yes, we must acknowledge and deal with our pain, but we must also acknowledge and embrace our blessings. Without acknowledging the gifts in our lives, we will remain hurt, angry, and empty, convinced we are among the unlucky ones. How can we receive when we aren't even conscious that we are being given to?

It is not surprising to me that the whole issue of abundance skips right over our heads. We don't learn about it in our homes; we don't learn about it in school. As we watch the news coverage each day, we are bombarded with rapes, murders, fires, and any other horror that happens to catch the attention of the news media. No talk of abundance here!

Although it is true that the teachings of our society tend to ignore the issue of gratitude, we all have the power to reverse the training, to teach ourselves how much there is to be grateful for in this world despite any negative circumstances that surround us. (Remember: We are not victims!) In so doing, we learn the secret of harvesting, of reaping the bounty that lies all around us.

When we harvest, we don't need to hang on so tightly to so many things—the past, the future, the shoulds, the way it's supposed to be, our expectations, and on and on and on. We can open our arms and let go, thus ending the struggle and dancing with life. It is important to understand that unless we harvest, unless we scoop in the rewards, we will always have the pain and fear of an unlived life. Remember,

It's not that beauty doesn't exist in our world, it's that we seldom seem to notice!

In the last chapter I talked about harvesting through the practices of looking mindfully and deeply. In this chapter, I want to show you another way to harvest your life. It is through the creation of RITUALS that celebrate the riches of life.

My good friend Rob Eichberg[2] introduced me to a beautiful ritual that fits this description. The first time I attended a dinner party at his house, I was baffled when he said, "Before we begin eating, let's resonate." Having no idea what he was talking about, I sat there with a look of "Huh?" on my face. Thankfully, he noticed my dumb expression and explained that we were to close our eyes and simply hold hands around the table. I didn't know why he wanted us to do this, but like all dutiful guests, I went along with the program. But once I closed my eyes and held hands with those seated next to me, I understood why he wanted us to do this.

I didn't know most of the people at the table, but after a minute or so of "resonating," I felt an enhanced sense of connection, caring, and blessing. Before this simple ritual, we were just people getting together for one of Rob's delicious meals. Afterward, I felt gratitude for the opportunity of spending an evening with such special people, for having such a good friend as Rob, for the wonderful food we were going to eat, for my health. And for the first time in a long time, I realized the great value inherent in simple rituals. They help us remember what we tend to forget—all that is wonderful in our lives. They help us remember our gifts, our purpose, and our connectedness with all things.

The idea of ritual has been virtually abandoned in modern times, and what a loss this is! Holidays such as Christmas and

Thanksgiving are meant to remind us of our blessings, but they seldom do. They have been turned into crass commercial opportunities and are often experienced as times of upset and obligation. Hence they have lost their purpose, which is to remind us of who we truly are, why we are here, and what there is to be grateful for.

But even when holidays do fulfill their purpose, they leave us with too many days in between—*the majority of our lives*—when we tend to forget our blessings, when we live in a state of emptiness and pettiness rather than fullness and transcendence. We need *daily* rituals to help us embrace the beauty and transcend what is painful in our lives.

In his wonderful book *Return of the Rishi*, Deepak Chopra tells us of the tremendous value of ritual in his native India. He describes the devotional act of puja, which is performed twice a day by the multitudes. The words are not religious; they are words of thanks that children learn in early childhood as they listen to their parents perform this beautiful ritual. The rewards of puja are many:

"Joining the puja at twilight in Haridwar was a reminder to live gladly, put into song. For the moment, I was joining the choir of India and forgetting my single voice. The shadows of the temples lengthened to the horizon and took the day away with them. The swollen green river turned dark in the night and more gentle in its flow, as if accepting our thanks and then rolling over to sleep."[3]

What a beautiful image! Chopra points out that this kind of ritual is "something enduring to hold close, something that won't wash away in the furious tides of change." For many in India, poverty reigns supreme. But this simple ritual of gratitude puts abundance into the lap of all who practice it.

Wouldn't it be wonderful if here, in our Western society, at 7:00 every morning and 7:00 every evening, the entire population—rich, poor, old, young, African American, Christian, Jew, Muslim, Hispanic, Italian, and on and on—took five minutes to close their eyes, unite as one people, and join the choir of thanks for the abundance we have been given. Wow! What a concept! I don't think this kind of ritual can be organized in the near future, but as the great poet Rumi said many years ago,

"There are hundreds of ways to kneel and kiss the ground."

So let's focus on just a few very simple ways that we can kneel and kiss the ground as an act of awareness of everything that is wonderful about our lives. These are just suggestions. As you read, let your creativity flow and invent your own rituals that have a deep meaning in your own life.

RENEW THE AGE-OLD TRADITION OF GIVING THANKS AT DINNERTIME. Simply saying, "I am thankful for the food I am about to eat," gives us a little pause before gulping down our food mindlessly and without appreciation. Or you might try Rob's ritual of "resonating" with your family and/or other dinner mates. Hold hands and let the blessings roll over you. Feel the grand energy of human connection.

In the beginning, until your ritual becomes habit, put a sign on your table as a reminder to do some form of thanksgiving before each meal. (How quickly we forget!) Remember,

> **We have to train ourselves to be appreciative; our present habit is to be unappreciative.**

FIND A "GRATITUDE BUDDY." As you get involved in the busyness of your daily life, it helps to have a friend who is your wake-up call. Commit to calling each other regularly to talk about the blessings in your lives. Does this sound stupid and far-fetched? Hardly! Look around and notice many people call each other every day to talk about the misery in their lives! All it takes is a change in focus! We need to transform our "complaint buddies" into "gratitude buddies," and if your present buddies won't go along with the program, find new buddies!

In the beginning, talking about the goodies in your life may be more difficult than you think. When you stop complaining, you may have many long silences in your conversations. Nothing to talk about! You will notice how much of your time is spent complaining about all that is wrong with your life—your boss, your kids, your mate, your health, the economy, and so on. But soon your weak habit of complaining will be replaced by the powerful habit of gratitude. Every time you hang up the phone you will feel energized and positive. What a beautiful way to build a friendship!

CREATE A "GRATITUDE GROUP." Most groups are formed to help us deal with problems in our life, which is certainly one way to go. I wonder what would happen if we attended a group that focused only on the beauty in our lives. Would many of our problems disappear automatically? They might, considering that most of our problems are created by a victim mentality, or the sense that we aren't getting, doing, or being enough!

By definition, a gratitude group would help us realize that we aren't victims and that we are powerful enough to change anything that isn't working in our lives. Gratitude dissolves upsets and grievances. Would we need therapy if we were constantly grateful? As David Reynolds reports,

> "I've never met a suffering neurotic person who was filled with gratitude."[4]

Wise observation! Your gratitude group could be just a few people getting together each week, pointing out to one another how much there really is to celebrate. Or this group could consist of 150, as did The Inside Edge, the group my husband and I belonged to in Los Angeles.[5] Once a week we met at a local restaurant for a 6:30 A.M. breakfast. A lot of us were not grateful for having to get up so early in the morning, but it was worth it.

What awaited us was a few hours of acknowledging one another, laughing, hugging, hearing inspirational stories from other members and invited speakers. My husband used to say that the week began on Tuesday morning, when our meetings were held. The few hours we spent with a group of people who, for that brief moment in time, were focused on all that was wonderful in their lives set us up for a beautiful week.

You can structure the format of your group any way you please. It could be a dinner meeting where everyone contributes something to the pot. The ritual of "breaking bread" together is beautiful indeed. Or it could be an after-dinner meeting where the primary focus is simply talking about the beauty in your lives.

As an additional boost to your positive state of mind, a few times a year create an appreciation party. Again, make it a potluck event with everyone coming to the party with food to contribute as well as stories of things to be grateful for. No complaining for the entire party! Wow! Most parties I've been to lately have been evenings of doom and gloom as people focus on the bad news of politics, their business, and so on.

If anyone gets the urge to complain, other party members can show how the negatives can be turned into positives. They do this, of course, in the spirit of caring, not righteousness or judgment. In this way, everyone gets to go home enriched and upbeat, knowing there is a lot to celebrate in their lives.

WAKE UP TO HAPPINESS. When you awaken each morning, you can shut out the negative chatter of the mind by playing an affirmation tape that helps you focus on the highest part of who you are, instead of the lowest part of who you are. As a start, I suggest you listen to *Inner Talk for a Confident Day* each morning for at least six weeks or until the ideas become firmly rooted in your body and mind.[6] Later, when you get the feel of Higher-Self thinking, you can create your own personal affirmation tape. Starting each day with thoughts of power and love is a guaranteed way of helping break up the Lower-Self habit of focusing on lack and creating the Higher-Self habit of focusing on beauty and higher purpose.

COLLECT QUOTATIONS THAT MAKE YOU FEEL GOOD. Many times throughout the day, we read or hear thoughts that trigger a shift in our consciousness. It's wonderful to collect them in a little book to place on our desks or bedside so that we can read them often. We get so much from an inspirational, insightful, or humorous quote. Most of the quotes in this book come from my own collection that I have gathered over the years. They have helped me transcend the petty by reminding me of the grandness and/or humor of it all.

CREATE A BOOK OF ABUNDANCE. This is a truly wonderful tool for reminding us of our blessings. As I explained in *Feel the Fear and Do It Anyway*, the Book of Abundance is simply a notebook that is meant to be placed at your bedside. Each night before you go to bed, jot down at least fifty wonderful things that happened to you that day. "Fifty things, Susan! I can hardly think of three!" Obviously you have not been looking mindfully and deeply at the blessings in your life. The purpose of this exercise is to help you do so.

In the beginning the exercise may take a LONG, LONG time. Soon, however, the blessings will pour easily into your mind and onto the paper. That is because you will find yourself spending a lot of the day LOOKING FOR the blessings in your life so that you will have some new items to include in your Book of Abundance each night. And you will find them! The benefits are obvious:

As we start looking for the good, our focus automatically is taken off the bad.

If we can make looking for the abundance a habit, just think how our lives will be transformed! Some of the items you can include are:

My car started. I am able to walk. I have food to eat. Someone paid me a compliment. My kids haven't gotten in any trouble today. I felt the sun's warmth on my face. I spoke to one of my best friends. The flowers are starting to bloom. I have hot water in my shower. I'm breathing. The sun came out.

The items in your Book of Abundance do not have to be splashes of brilliance. In fact, it is better if they are not. Always keep in mind that if we focus only on the splashes of brilliance, we are left with "a life of boredom interjected with a few exquisite moments." One of our goals is to *make each moment exquisite*. We do this by acknowledging the gifts inherent in all the so-called ordinary events in our life. As we look at them mindfully and deeply, we begin to realize that these ordinary moments aren't ordinary at all—they are extraordinary! Take breathing, for example. Isn't it incredibly, wildly, extraordinary! St. Augustine reminds us,

"People travel to wonder at the height of mountains, at the huge waves of the sea, at the long courses of rivers, at the vast compass of the ocean, at the circular motion of the stars . . . and they pass by themselves without wondering."

Amazing, isn't it, that we miss the greatest miracles of all when we focus only on the obvious grand splashes that are hard to miss. *So much would be added to our lives if we learned how to revel in the incredible gifts inherent in the ordinary.*

As you write your list in your Book of Abundance, don't forget to look mindfully and deeply at each item. Don't just pass over them as you write. Embrace them! As you fall off to sleep, you will hold this abundance in your heart. By the way, can you imagine what a positive effect this would have if you did this exercise with your children? Perhaps they would derive, at an early age, the happiness, fullness, and abundance that has eluded you up until now.

CREATE A GOOD-NIGHT REMINDER. Each night before you go to sleep, create a word or two that embodies a sense of appreciation for all that has been given to you during the day. And as you close your eyes to go off to sleep, keep repeating the word or words you have selected for the evening. Very often, I fall asleep to the words "thank you." This simple ritual keeps me from dwelling on annoying and petty daily events that would ordinarily keep me awake. But as I keep repeating "thank you," I am soon peacefully asleep. Any of the following words might work for you:

embrace, breathe, trust, open, heal, lighten, enjoy, delight, appreciate, care, share, enough, savor, receive, let go, touch, flow

Affirmations work as well, such as,

> **I am at peace.**
> **I trust.**
> **I am blessed.**
> **I am loved.**
> **I love.**

Blessed sleep will come much more quickly with such nourishing, healing, loving thoughts.

**COUNT THE MANY SHOULDERS YOU ARE
STANDING ON.** Noah benShea tells us a very relevant
story. A little boy goes to a parade with his father. In order
for the little boy to see, his father hoists him up on his
shoulders. As the parade passes by, the little boy keeps
telling his father how spectacular are the passing sights. Unfortunately, he gets so arrogant about his wonderful view
that he mocks those who see less: "If only you could see
what I can see . . ." But what the boy doesn't see was WHY
he could see. BenShea points out that the boy could have
been a giant:

> "A giant . . . is anyone who remembers we are all
> sitting on someone else's shoulder."[7]

He reminds us what we are if we don't remember—a
BURDEN! When I read that, it made me cringe. How
many times have I not remembered whose shoulder I was
standing on? How many times did I not thank those who
had contributed greatly to my life? How many times was I a
burden instead of a giant?

We can all learn to be giants instead of burdens with
the simple ritual of writing down each day one or more
people whose shoulders we are standing upon. We will
never run out of people to include. Not only can we list significant others (parents, siblings, children, mates) but also
the "invisible" people who work very hard to make our
lives better.

These invisible people include garbage collectors, bus
drivers, farmers, factory workers, waiters and waitresses,
postal workers, government workers, and all those who
make our lives run more smoothly whom we somehow take
for granted. Be as specific as you can. For example, "the

waitress who served me my breakfast, the farmer who grew that wonderful tomato on my sandwich, my son who sent me a thank-you note," and so on.

We can even include things on our list—our car for taking us where we need to go, the water that sustains our life, the clothes that warm our body, the air we breathe. We are best served when we don't take *anything* for granted! A side benefit is that as we stop taking things for granted, we begin to love and take better care of the things that support our life on this planet.

You really begin to stand tall when you realize how many shoulders you are standing on; you also feel richer in spirit. And just as important, you are less of a burden and more of a giant as you acknowledge the contribution that others make to your life.

Noah benShea's little story makes us think twice about the concept of the "self-made" man or woman. If you think you are self-made, think again. Your parents clothed, fed, and took care of you. Your teachers educated you. Your boss hired you. Your customers supported your business efforts. Your suppliers helped you deliver the goods. Your phone and fax helped you set up the business. Your employees kept the business going. Or whatever it is for you. These are just obvious ways you were supported. What about the air you breathe, or the house you live in, or the food you eat, and on and on and on. Are you *sure* you are self-made?

The truth is that when we look back on all our achievements, we see that we have done NOTHING on our own. That should humble us a bit! In fact, the more appreciative we become, the more humble we become, which is a good thing. Arrogance is very hard to live with, whether it's in others or in ourselves. We also feel less impoverished or a victim when we are aware of all the blessings we receive from other people in our world. When we have this awareness, we feel part of a larger whole, a network of caring, a network of people standing on each other's shoulders. How blessed we are.

CULTIVATE THE HABIT OF SAYING "THANK YOU." The next ritual follows naturally from the last, and that is to cultivate the habit of verbalizing our thanks. When we look mindfully and deeply at the beauty in our lives, and begin to list the multitude of people and things who have supported us in the past and support us in the present, there can be only two words that come from our heart and to our lips, and these words are . . .

THANK YOU!

The inclusion of the words THANK YOU in our vocabulary sets up an interesting paradox. Each time we say these two powerful words, we are acknowledging a gift we were given. By definition, if we say THANK YOU often enough, any trace of a poverty consciousness disappears; we begin feeling incredibly abundant.

On the other hand, if we don't say THANK YOU very often, it is a sign we are taking things for granted. When we take things for granted, we are sleepwalking our way through life. Giving thanks is one way of waking ourselves up. And speaking of waking up, the morning is a wonderful time to begin your process of saying thanks. What have you got to thank so early in the morning?

"Thank you, body, for keeping me alive. Thank you, coffee, for the delicious wake-up call. Thank you, vitamins and breakfast, for nourishing me. Thank you, hot shower, for the luscious feeling of warmth and comfort. Thank you, house, for protecting me from the elements. Thank you, makeup and hair dryer, shaver and comb, for helping me feel ready to face the day. Thank you, car, for starting.* Thank you, roads, stop signs, traffic lights, for getting me to work safely. Thank you, job, for giving me money to buy what I need."

And I only skimmed the surface. What if you looked deeply as I described in the last chapter at each of these items. You'd be saying thank you all day! You may think it's ridiculous to think of such ordinary things in our lives as blessings. But what if you didn't have them? In his poignant story about life in a concentration camp, Viktor Frankl tells us that it is just these kinds of ordinary things that he and the other men missed.

> "In my mind I took bus rides, unlocked the front door of my apartment, answered my telephone, switched on the electric lights. Our thoughts often centered on such details, and these memories could move one to tears."[8]

Here are people who had everything taken away and were surrounded by unimaginable horrors, and their thoughts went to all the little things we so callously take for granted.

Not only do we take things for granted, we take people for granted. Our thanks to them is incredibly important, particularly to those who are most significant in our lives. Although it may be easier (when we remember) to thank the bus driver, the waitress, the toll booth collector, the garbage collector, and so on, it is sometimes very difficult to thank those who are significant in our lives—our parents, our mates, our children, and even our boss and coworkers.

For example, when I was single, I found it very difficult

---

*We never seem to thank our car for the 364 days it is running; we notice only the one day it isn't. The same thing holds for most things in our life!

to thank the men I dated. For a number of reasons, I didn't want to acknowledge the gifts they brought into my life. In the first place, I used to be a very angry woman. It is difficult for angry people to say thank you. They'd rather have their teeth pulled! As I got rid of my anger, the thanks came pouring out of me. I even phoned old boyfriends and thanked them for all that they had given me that I never thanked them for before. Some of them cried; they weren't used to being thanked.

It's also difficult to say thanks when we are afraid of being dependent on anyone, or obligated to anyone. This is the time to FEEL THE FEAR AND SAY THANKS ANY-WAY! Also, many of us find it difficult to say thank you because we think we give much more than we receive. Sometimes this is true. And I'm not someone who finds footprints on the face very attractive. But sometimes we think we are giving more than we get simply because *we fail to notice how much we are given.*

For example, there are so many of us who blame our parents for all the ills of our lives. What is there to thank them for? We forget that they fed us, clothed us, changed our dirty diapers, paid for doctors and dentists—often when they didn't feel like it. However they may have handled their role as parents, we owe our survival to them.

We also tend to forget the upset *we've caused them*—the times we were ill, or late coming home from school, or crying in the middle of the night, or critical and unapprecia-tive of all that we were given. I love the joke about three little old ladies talking. The first said she had two children. The second said she had three children. The third said she had no children. "No children!", said the first. "What do you do for aggravation?" (You parents out there understand exactly what she was talking about!) Yes, we sometimes cre-ated much aggravation for those who loved us as we were growing up, and it's time that we "knelt and kissed the ground" in thanks for our parents.

I know that if our parents were mentally or physically abusive as we were growing up, saying thanks seems like an act of absurdity. Why thank them for anything? I'll tell you why. As I explained in Chapter 7, the victim mentality is a form of SELF-abuse. It takes away all the joy in living. Why trade one form of abuse for another? Blame is a function of our Lower Self. In order to truly end the struggle and dance with life, it is necessary to get off of the syndrome of blame.

One of the ways we can do this is to rise to the level of the Higher Self and focus on the gifts our parents have given us—most important, the gift of life—and then express our thanks. Take the time really to look deeply and mindfully at the process of parenting and find those acts of giving, even sacrifice, on the part of your parents for which you can be truly grateful. Trust me when I say YOU OWE THIS TO YOURSELF! Gratitude is one of the most powerful ways of healing the many understandable hurts that may be hampering your ability truly to enjoy your life.

Yes, saying thank you can be a very difficult thing to do. In a world encased in upset and struggle, it seems easier to say HELP! But begin the practice now. At least ten times a day say thank you to people in your life. You can't imagine how much these little words will contribute to your sense of gratitude and well-being—and the well-being of others.

FIND WAYS TO GIVE IN RETURN. Albert Einstein once said:

> "A hundred times a day I remind myself that my inner and outer life depends on the labors of other men, living and dead, and that I must exert myself

in order to give in the full measure I have received and am still receiving."

When our hearts are filled with gratitude, we feel a deep desire to give back to the Universe and the people around us. Some of us may feel guilty when we realize how much we have taken without giving anything in return. I see this as a healthy guilt, if there is such a thing. As you begin giving back, the guilt disappears and is replaced by a feeling of incredible well-being. As we realize that we are a meaningful part of the world around us, the circle of connection and belonging is completed. This feels very good indeed!

What also happens as we begin to give back is that our behavior begins to mirror our appreciation. We lose our temper less, we care more about the state of the environment, we don't waste as much, we don't need as much, we are kinder to others. Gratitude has many ripple effects in making ours a wonderful world.

So make it a daily ritual to include one pay-back item on your daily to-do list—whether it's picking up paper that's cluttering the street, or contributing time or money to one of your favorite charities, or writing a letter of thanks, or buying a gift for someone, or whatever. As you begin the process of paying back, you begin to feel better and better about yourself. Nothing creates a greater sense of self than recognizing that you are a truly meaningful part of your family, your community, your country, and this planet.

You get the picture. I'm sure you can think of many, many ways to create rituals for noticing the abundance in your life and giving thanks. Your goal is to make gratitude your normal way of approaching life, and this takes a lot of practice. You may feel that you have no time for practice. Understand that although the occasional retreat or vacation or workshop has much to offer in terms of helping us develop Higher-Self practices, the *real* practice is done in our ordinary lives—raising our children, going to work, driving in the country, and the multitude of other activities that barely get our attention.

Instead of saying you can't practice gratitude because you have to take care of the children, use the caring of the children for your practice of gratitude. If your time is spent largely at work, use your work for the practice of gratitude. I understand that it's easier to pay attention to our blessings lying on a beach during a summer holiday. It's another thing to remember them in a traffic jam! But the practice of gratitude is meant to be done in our everyday lives, not in the abstract. Believe me, all the practice is well worth it. Remember that . . .

As your awareness of the riches available to you in your everyday life grows, you are on the way to becoming the laughing Buddha. Life is joyous. Life is light. Life is happy. You are awake at last.

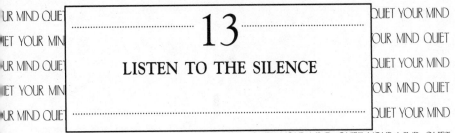

13

LISTEN TO THE SILENCE

Listen to the silence . . .

It has much to say.

Susan Jeffers

Y

EARS AGO I SAW A TINY FRAMED
poster of an inviting forest of aspen trees. I was attracted to the caption, which said simply,

"When you come upon a magic place, listen."

The symbolism of this important tidbit of wisdom escaped me at the time, even though I knew there was something within it that I needed to learn.

At first, I thought the message was solely about going into nature. But as time went on, I realized that the deeper essence of the message was that in order to embrace fully the riches in our life, we need to go deep within our being to our Higher Self—and beyond—and listen to the important messages we hold inside. In order to do this, we must learn how to embrace the silence, how to quiet the endless chatter in the mind, the chatter of the Lower Self, so that we can hear.

Yet quieting the mind is easier said than done. It was Bertolt Brecht who gave us the image of "lying in the meadow, and dangling with my soul." *Can you remember the last time you allowed yourself such moments of silent wonder?* If you are anything like the rest of us, the answer is NO.

Silence is a no-no in our society, so there are very few of us who have embraced the riches of a quiet mind. A child lying on the bed doing nothing is often greeted by a nagging parent's insistence that he or she get up and *do* something. What we don't realize is that the

166

child *is* doing something, something very important—connecting with the solitude.

We do such a disservice to our children—and ourselves—by filling every moment with activity. We have been much too influenced by our forefathers who believed that idleness was a sin. Thomas Jefferson once said, "Determine never to be idle. It is wonderful how much may be done if we are always doing." I suspect he was a driven, obsessive man and didn't spend one moment "dangling with his soul"! Poor thing!

Because it's a rarity, most of us are uncomfortable with silence. The moment we enter our homes, the television goes on or we pick up the phone—or both. The minute we get into our cars, the radio or tape machines goes on. Silence is, indeed, a scary prospect for many people who *need* noise or busyness around them all the time.

Despite our discomfort with silence, I believe that we all have a yearning to get to this peaceful place within our being. In his ultimate wisdom Henry David Thoreau once said:

"Many men go fishing all of their lives without knowing that it is not fish they are after."

In the end, what they are after is a sense of quiet, appreciation, and peace that is missing in their lives. Let me explore with you a very powerful way of reaching and ultimately embracing the silence of your mind, thus transforming your experience of life from one of confusion and clutter into one of peaceful awareness—MEDITATION.

Many of us don't like the concept of meditation. It conjures up pictures of people sitting in a monastery in the crossed-legged lotus position being quiet for days on end. Yes, there are those who meditate that way. But for most of us in Western civilization, this is neither practical nor appealing. Luckily, there are other options.

One of the most popular of these options is called TRANSCENDENTAL MEDITATION (TM for short). It was brought to the United States in 1959 by a monk from India, Maharishi Mahesh Yogi. Yet it is important to keep in mind that . . .

TM has nothing to do with religion. It's not even a philosophy or a suggested lifestyle. TM is purely a *mechanical* technique for achieving a deep state of restful awareness.[1]

So don't let any religious considerations stop you from deriving all the potential benefits from TM. It is the most studied form of meditation and the documented value it gives to our lives is enormous.

Because TM can be used by everyone, it has been adopted by many people in the mainstream—bankers, college students, athletes, grocery clerks, teachers, and so on. TM has achieved its popularity for a number of reasons.

TM is very easy to do. All it requires is that we sit comfortably in a chair, with our eyes closed, silently repeating to ourselves a meaningless word (mantra) given to us by an instructor. This gently pulls our mind into a state of peaceful alertness and awareness. TM can be practiced anywhere—riding in a bus, in your office, sitting in bed. It's very portable.

TM offers us a deeper state of rest than sleep. When we include in a hectic day short periods of rest that are deeper than sleep, the quality of our lives improves enormously![2]

TM is great for our health. According to many health professionals, TM is good for just about everything that ails us. As a result, it is regularly used and prescribed by doctors all over the world. In these health-conscious times, it makes perfect sense to learn TM and to include it in our daily lives, not only to heal illness but to prevent it as well. TM also is known to retard the aging process. A wonderful incentive!

TM improves our mental abilities. Dr. Christopher Hegarty, a nationally renowned management consultant, said:

"I consider the TM program to be the single most effective technique available for developing this optimum level of mental competence."

He states that it gives us access to our own deepest resources, "what I have found to be an unlimited reservoir of inner energy and creative intelligence."[3] Gertrude Stein was right on target when she said:

"It takes a lot of time to be a genius. You have to sit around so much doing nothing, really doing nothing."

TM improves our emotional state, hence, our relationships with everyone in our lives. TM helps us let go of negative emotions that take away our joy in life, emotions such as anger, fear, depression, anxiety, and the like. As a result we become much calmer and more enjoyable to be around. This makes us better parents, spouses, members of the workforce, and so on. Most important, we are in a much better place to end the struggle and dance with life.

TM even reduces crime. In a number of studies, it was found that when only 1 percent of the population practiced TM, the crime rate dropped significantly. Amazing! I know many of you are sitting there with a great deal of skepticism about this. (It was initially hard for me to take in as well!) But TM's positive effect on crime has been verified by outside review panels that concluded that as more people meditate, the negative tendencies in society decline.

The TM explanation for this is that at a very deep level, we are connected as one energy. (Quantum physics is certainly agreeing with this notion.) If that energy is negative, the negativity spreads throughout the community. If that energy is positive, the positive energy spreads throughout the community. If you think about how violence seems to be spreading out of control in our society right now, this makes perfect sense. We definitely need a positive antidote, and TM seems to fit the bill.

The reported benefits of TM go on and on. It makes one wonder, "How does meditation work?" Leon Weiner, my TM instructor,[4] used the analogy of water. When water is in high activity, it boils, it's volatile. If you reduce the activity, a sense of calm comes over the water. So too when we reduce the activity in our mind—a sense of calm comes over our being. The intermittent silent repetition of our *mantra*, which is chosen because of its sound, is a very effective device to help stop the volatility of the mind. It also gives the mind something to hold on to and gently leads it to calmer spaces.

And so our mind is calm. What's the big deal? What is there to gain? How about happiness, peace, energy, creativity, intelligence, intuition, guidance, health, orderliness, joy, and all good things? A feeling of calm is our way into the Higher Self, the best of who we are. It is also our way into a Universal oneness with all there is.

As we touch this place within our being over and over again, our relationships with all things begin to change for the better. In the beginning we don't feel much change, but over time the effects are extraordinary. Leon explained it to me this way:

Imagine we are dying a white piece of cloth in a vat of beet juice. We soak it for a while until it takes on the color of the beet juice, and then we hang it in the sun to dry. Eventually the cloth fades to a very faint pink. We do this again, and we notice our piece of cloth again fades but not quite as much as the first time. As we repeat this process over and over and over again, there comes a time when the cloth seems to hold the richness of its color.

So too with meditation. Each time we dip down into the abundance of our inner being, we emerge a little richer. Over time, the whole quality of our life is improved in a magnificent way.

This was a brief introduction to TM. You may want to look into other forms of meditation such as Buddhist meditation or Mindfulness meditation. *TM is just one of many highly effective possibilities.* Check out the different options. Your local bookstore will most likely have many books and audiotapes about meditation that will help you decide which is best for you.

Another possibility is simply to sit in silence for fifteen or twenty minutes a day. The renowned Louise Hay makes it a practice of sitting quietly, closing her eyes, taking a deep breath, and asking, "What is it I need to know?" And then she listens.[5] Judging from her many contributions to this world, she gets wonderful answers indeed!

Some people use chanting to get them into a meditative state. Others use guided visualizations (such as the one I provided in Chapter 6), which have proven very valuable to me.[6] Scan the bulletin boards of your local spiritually oriented bookstores to see if any classes are available that teach you how to get into a meditative state. The point is to find something that works for *you*.

Whatever the method, the purpose of quieting the mind is always the same—to step out of our own way and touch a Universal oneness with all things.

In the beginning, sitting in the silence may be uncomfortable. But after a while, we come to look forward to this wondrous time where we have NOTHING to do but be there. In this time of increased struggle and responsibility, what could be better? In the beginning you may fall asleep. That's perfectly okay. Or you may daydream. That's perfectly okay. Or you may be bored. That's perfectly okay. Isn't it wonderful to do something where whatever you do is perfectly okay?

Some people try to empty their minds totally and resist the thoughts that come up as they meditate. My experience is that thoughts always come up as you meditate. It's simply the nature of the mind. Meditation helps us learn that *thoughts are just thoughts, and we don't have to get attached to the drama they can bring.* In meditation, we watch our thoughts passing by as if they were floats in a parade or clouds passing by on a sunny day. We become the witness instead of the central figure in the drama. In so doing we are totally changing our relationship with the thoughts that usually drive us crazy.

It's important to make time for meditation once you've chosen a technique that works for you, and that may be the biggest hurdle of all. It's tough to get into the routine. I speak from experience on that one. But you would be wise to make it a priority in your life. As Hugh and Gayle Prather suggest, *give it the same priority you give to diarrhea!*[7] It's that important!

Many people create separate spaces in their homes for the purposes of meditation. This is not necessary, but it does help to get us in the mood. A little ritual helps to set the stage as well. I love to light a candle as I begin to meditate. It reminds me of the Light that shines within my being. And it says to the chatter in my mind, "You better settle down now." Needless to say, we need all the help we can get to quiet the chatter in the mind.

I know that in many ways it is difficult, if not impossible, truly to understand how meditation works. To a logical mind, it makes no sense whatsoever. As Stuart Wilde reminds us, the mind will try to pull you away with logic. But remember,

"Logic is death to that part of you that is the miracle maker."[8]

Meditation is a way of really sinking our roots deeply into the source of our being. Although it is wonderful to learn about life from books, tapes, and all manner of external teachers, if that is the only source of our learning, we are what Krishnamurti calls "second-hand people."[9] When we go to the source that lies deep within our being to guide us in our Journey through life, we become firsthand people once again.

Rule of thumb: When something is deeply troubling you, just sit with it. Don't do anything. Listen to the wisdom within your being. Eventually you will get the answers you are seeking. In the emptiness, all things fall into place. It is a strange paradox that in emptying the mind, we find exquisite fullness. This wonderful quote from Franz Kafka written a long time ago inspires us:

> "You do not need to leave your room. Remain sitting at your table and listen. Do not even listen, simply wait. Do not even wait, be quite still and solitary. The world will freely offer itself to you to be unmasked, it has no choice, it will roll in ecstasy at your feet."[10]

As we turn off the sound and move into silence, the dancing can begin. We finally hear the music of our Soul, and it is this that gives us peace. And as we listen to the music of our Soul, we mysteriously and wondrously hear the music of everyone else's as well . . . and we are one with the world.

14

TALK TO THE CHIEF

WHAT COULD GIVE US AS MUCH peace as meditation? The answer is PRAYER. Actually, prayer is often characterized as a form of meditation. Prayer can be a wonderful way to transcend the petty and bring peace to a struggling mind.

Perhaps you are someone who does not believe in God or a Higher Power. I suggest that you pray anyway. The healing effects of prayer, *even for those who do not believe in God,* have been documented in a number of scientific studies and it is hard to deny the evidence.[1] So pray to the Spirit or Higher Self within or simply to the grand mystery of it all. But don't negate the potential power of prayer in your life. It can be an awesome force indeed.

There are many ways that people pray. Although there is no right or wrong way to pray, I believe that some prayers can create confusion and distrust whereas others can create an incredible sense of power and love. Needless to say, it's important to learn the difference!

When I was a little girl, I used to say the same prayer every night:

"Dear God. Please let my mommy and daddy live forever."

Well, my mommy and daddy didn't live forever. One could say that God let me down. But I've learned a lot since then, and I know that God didn't let me down at all. I just asked amiss. I didn't really understand how to pray in a way that is *guaranteed* to bring me all that I ask for and need. My lack of understanding was bound to bring me disappointment and heartache.

The question is, "How many of us have grown beyond the level of the child when it comes to prayer?" I suspect very few of us. For example, I suspect that some form of the following prayer sounds familiar to many single women today:

Dear God. I am getting older. Please send me a wonderful man to marry so I can begin my family within one year.

I'll also wager that a good number of these women insert some adjectives in their prayer such as handsome, rich, and generous. (I'm sure that many single men have an equivalent prayer!) Some of us pray that our loved ones get well when they are ill or that we find a job when money is short or that a certain business venture turns out successfully or that we win the lottery, and so on.

Some of us are needy and beg God to give us what we feel we can't provide for ourselves. Our prayers sound something like, "HELP! BAIL ME OUT!" Others are more arrogant. We think we know *exactly* what is right for us and we ask God to be our delivery boy. Our prayers sound something like . . .

"Let me have that job. I know it is perfect for me."

To make matters worse, not only do we ask God to do it for us, we then worry that He (or She) won't do it *right!* Does this sound familiar? I'm here to tell you that . . .

Any time we are asking God to fill our order, we are setting ourselves up for disappointment!

Prayers such as the above—those that ask for something—are often called "petitionary prayers." I believe that we set ourselves up for an immense amount of fear, anger, disappointment, and all sorts of other negative emotions when we pray in this way. Petitionary prayers do not do the job of ending our struggle—whether they have loving sentiments behind them or selfish ones. The simple reason for this is that *sometimes they are answered and sometimes they are not.*

Sometimes we get the job; sometimes we don't. Sometimes our loved ones get well; sometimes they don't. Sometimes our business is successful; sometimes it isn't. Sometimes we find the man or woman to marry; sometimes we don't.

As a result we are left with very little peace of mind as we worry, or even obsess, about the outcome of important situations in our lives.

By definition, petitionary prayers have *expectations* behind them, and I've already discussed the suffering that results from expectations. Even though petitionary prayers sometimes "work," they offer no guarantees. If our prayers are not answered, we can't help but feel disappointed, or even betrayed.

Given all this, let me offer you three other types of prayer that bring us the peace of mind we are seeking *every time we pray*. You will see how vastly they differ from petitionary prayer.

PRAYERS OF TRUST

I spend a lot of my time teaching people across the country how to deal with their fears. Toward the end of each class, I ask my students, "How many of you believe in God?" Almost everyone raises his or her hand. I then ask the question, "Then why are you afraid?" And there is a stunned look on many of their faces. Others nod and smile as they recognize the crux of the problem. I point out that obviously *they hold God in their heads, but they don't hold God in their hearts*. They don't *trust* the ability of the Divine energy to lead them in the "right" direction.

By definition, petitionary prayers say that we don't trust the Grand Design. We don't trust the rhyme or reason for things that happen in our lives and in the lives of others we care about. We don't trust the great wisdom of the Universe. We ask for things to be OUR way, not God's way.

We play God when our need is really to trust God.

Prayers of trust can teach us to hold God in our hearts where the fear disappears and the peace of mind begins. Trust in a Higher Power (and trust in ourselves) are clearly the missing elements in a society filled with struggle.

In Chapter 6 I stressed the importance of learning how to turn things over to our Higher Selves when we are feeling a sense of struggle. This is trusting ourselves. Turning things over to a Higher Power is simply an extension of this process. As I experience it, *the Higher Self is the conduit to a Higher Power.*

Therefore, at those times when we are able to trust and "feel" God as a force in our lives, we are most certainly in the realm of our Higher Self. In the same vein, when we turn things over to our Higher Selves, we are also touching the realm of a Higher Power. When our prayers don't seem to "work," it is a surety we are praying from the fearful and insecure realm of the Lower Self, the place from which petitionary prayers usually arise. From this place, we are definitely asking amiss.

Given all this, what does a prayer of trust—a prayer that touches the Higher Self—sound like? The following is a good example:

> **"Dear God. I trust that no matter what happens in my life, it is for my highest good. And no matter what happens in the lives of those I love, it is for their highest good. From all things that are put before us all, we shall become stronger and more loving people."**

How powerful this kind of prayer is! It asks for nothing. It has no attachment behind it. It says that even if I don't find that man, even if I don't get that job, even if my loved one doesn't get well, I know that whatever happens is for the highest good of all concerned.

This isn't just a rationalization to make us feel better. As I said earlier, the "unwanted" situations in my life, such as my bout with cancer and my divorce, ultimately enriched me immeasurably. As a result, I have learned to have much more trust in the Grand Design. This kind of trust helps me let go and stop trying to control all that happens to me in life. In more and more situations, I find myself saying, "Okay, God, take over now."

Understand that turning matters over to our Higher Selves or a Higher Power, whatever that is for you, is not a way to abdicate responsibility. It is simply having the trust that, *when we have done our best*, the future will all happen perfectly.

PRAYERS OF GRATITUDE

I recently heard the following little rhyme, which I think is very appropriate here:

"Giving again?" I asked in dismay. "Must I keep giving time and money away?" "No," said the Angel piercing me through. "Just give until God stops giving to you."

If God were human, He (or She) would have an incredible inferiority complex. As I pointed out in Chapter 11, so much is given to us and so little is appreciated. Infusing our prayers with gratitude is a wonderful way to notice all that we have been given. When we are grateful, peace enters our hearts and our neediness abates. As far as I am concerned,

Seeing the abundance around us *is* seeing God. If we don't see the abundance in our lives, by definition, we have lost sight of God.

What does a prayer of gratitude sound like? It's very simple:

"I am grateful for all the beauty and opportunity you put into my life. And in all that I do, I shall seek to be a channel for your love."

Again, see how differently this touches our Heart when compared with a petitionary prayer. This prayer says, "I am aware of your gen-

erosity, and I will share it with everyone I meet." A prayer of gratitude makes us see all things anew.

When we put our prayer of trust together with our prayer of
gratitude, we get a powerful prayer indeed.

> **"Dear God. I trust that no matter what happens in my
> life, it is for my highest good. And no matter what hap-
> pens in the lives of those I love, it is for their highest
> good. From all things that are put before us, we shall be-
> come stronger and more loving people. I am grateful for
> all the beauty and opportunity you put into my life. And
> in all that I do, I shall seek to be a channel for your love."**

Take this prayer into your heart and notice the struggle abating and
the peace entering your being.

PRAYERS OF COMMUNION

Prayers of communion need not have any words. They are simply
about being in the presence of the radiant Spirit of a Higher Power.
In this place, the feeling of being lost in the world totally vanishes.
We are Home and we are safe.

My personal vision of a Higher Power—and I suspect everyone's
vision is different—is one of Universal Light that I can tap into and
commune with at will. I often enter this vibrant state of silent
prayer through the following visualization:

> I breathe in deeply and then imagine myself breathing out
> through a large opening at the top of my head into a vast
> sky of luminous healing light. Next I imagine myself breath-
> ing back in some of this luminous healing light through the
> opening at the top of my head until it fills up my entire body
> from head to toe. Then I imagine myself breathing out, ra-
> diating this Universal Light out into the world through my
> breath and through every pore in my body, touching every-

thing as far and as wide as my mind can see. I then breathe into my being the Light from all the world around me.

As I repeat this process over and over again, I feel a wonderful cyclical connection between the Universal Light, my entire being, and the rest of the world. It gives me an incredible feeling of peace and radiance in a very short time. My thoughts are calmed, and I feel myself a very powerful and loving being. I am touched by a Divine Radiance. I have the reassuring sense that I am part of something much bigger than my limited mind allows me to understand. I am connected. I belong to all things.

When in this beautiful state of being, the concerns of the earthly plane are diminished immensely. I am connected to an unbelievable sweetness. Over time, I have learned that, despite what is happening in my life, this haven of luminous power is always there for me, as it is there for everyone. All we have to do is create our own means of tapping into it and embracing it.

When we are sitting in communion with God we are not asking for anything to be different from the way it is. We are allowing all things to be "all all right" exactly as they are. We are "letting go and letting God" as the saying goes. When we are in this space, we know there is nothing else to "get"; hence, there is nothing to ask for!

When we pray regularly—using prayers of trust, appreciation, communion, or whatever works for you[2]—the benefits ultimately spill over into all areas of our lives. We come to realize that the Universal Light and Spirit of God is with us at all times, no matter what is happening at any given moment. We need only to tap into this Divine Presence to find an exquisite piece of "Heaven" that we can take into our hearts and radiate out to everyone whose life touches ours. In this place, our fear disappears and is replaced by an intense sense of love and caring.

I ask you—could it be that something as simple as prayer could ultimately be the force that heals the world? I wouldn't be surprised!

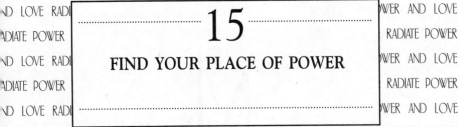

15

FIND YOUR PLACE OF POWER

M ANY YEARS AGO I WAS ON A sailboat in the Caribbean. The owners of the sailboat were John and his fiancée, new friends I had made on my two-week vacation. In John's effort to show me a wonderful time (or test my courage!), he set sail at dusk for a neighboring island where we were going to spend the night. It didn't bother him that it was almost dark and the seas were incredibly rough, but it sure bothered me!

As the sails were hoisted and we were in open seas, I found myself being rocked wildly from side to side. I tried very hard to steady both the sea and the boat, but needless to say, neither would cooperate. I sat rigidly on the bench lining the left side of the boat, resisting each up-and-down motion and feeling seasickness quickly come upon me. I decided this would never do. I had to try another approach.

Somewhere within me I had the presence to stand up and fight my way to the center of the deck on which I had been sitting. I then faced forward and steadied myself by placing the palms of my hands onto a waist-high storage box that was secured to the deck. I clearly remember making the decision to let go of my resistance and to surrender to the movement below my feet and to *anything* that might befall us on our journey in the little boat. It was a "Take over, Universe!" kind of feeling.

I soon felt loose, free, and strangely at peace, a far cry from the place of fear, resistance, and rigidity in which I had been just a few moments before. Having reached what I now recognize as a Higher-Self state, it took only a matter of moments to discover what the concept of sea legs was all about. Instead of fighting the turbulence, I went *with* it, allowing my legs to move up and down with the motion of the boat. The result was that my torso (my center) remained steady while my legs were beautifully riding the sea.

Picture this in your mind. When the left side of the boat went up, I shifted my weight to my right leg, allowing my left leg to move with the rise of the boat. And when the right side of the boat went up, I shifted my weight to my left leg, allowing my right leg to move with the rise of the boat. By just shifting my weight to accommodate the movement of the boat, I created an incredible sense of flow. The sea, the boat, and I had become one. Seasickness does not exist in such an exalted state of flow. Talk about a natural high! Talk about exquisite moments!

To feel calm in the midst of turbulence is a remarkable state indeed!

As it turned out, my joyful and amazingly peaceful state of mind turned out to be a very good thing. The fog began to settle in, and John, to his great embarrassment, lost his way. At this point I was actually calmer than he was. And ultimately, it was I who spotted the light shining faintly from the lighthouse, which ultimately led us to our harbor of safety. What is significant is that . . .

By simply shifting my relationship to all that was around me, I was able to turn misery into ecstasy—Hell into Heaven.

What could have been one of the most horrific evenings of my life turned into one of the most sublime.

Over the years I have asked myself how we could acquire something as wondrous as sea legs in our everyday lives, how we could shift our relationship to all that is around us to create a sense of calm when everything around us is chaotic. If we learned that, we would have come a long way toward ending the struggle and dancing with life.

The closest I've come to finding an answer has to do with the art of CENTERING. As I see it, centering is a process that allows the body and mind to align with the Higher Self, which is exactly what I experienced on John's boat. When our body and mind are out of alignment with our Higher Self, we are easily toppled over, out of balance. Hence, our task seems clear: We need to learn the tools for helping us to create this magical alignment.

Although the concept of centering may be hard at first to grasp, understand that all the tools I've offered in this book and my previous books help us achieve a centered state. They are tools for shifting our relationship with everything around us. For example, when we use affirmations or visualizations, we are coming back to center. When we meditate or pray, we are coming back to center. When we say YES to our Universe, we are coming back to center. When we cut the imaginary umbilical cord with others in our lives, we are coming back to center. When we ask ourselves "What if this were all all right?" we are coming back to center. And so on. *We are taking back our power.* We are not allowing the outside world to affect our stability or our happiness. Valuable tools indeed!

If you notice, these are all tools that help the MIND align with the Higher Self. Using these tools consistently, we can learn to think in a way that centers us, thereby increasing our sense of inner power and flow and our connection to the world around us. This is in contrast to our thinking in a way that fragments us, thus creating a sense of helplessness and fear.

There are also some marvelous tools for bringing our BODY in alignment with our Higher Self. Going back to my experience in the sailboat, simply shifting my body's relationship to the boat and the sea gave me the sea legs necessary to weather the storm. So too in life, we can learn ways of centering our body so that we walk, stand, and sit in a way that keeps us powerful within our being. These tools for physical centering give us an immense amount of rootedness that keeps us steady in times of turmoil.

A wonderful demonstration of the power we gain from physical centering was shown to a group of us by martial arts expert Tom Crum. He asked two strong men to come forward, one standing to the left of him, the other standing to the right. He asked them to hold the elbows of his bent arms and try to lift him. They did so with great ease as they were much bigger than Tom and appeared to be much stronger as well.

Next he told us he was going to "center himself," which we learned was a process that takes a mere second in time and is invisible to the naked eye. He then asked the two men to try and lift him again. We were all amazed as they stressed and strained but found it impossible to pick him up off the ground!

Obviously, it wasn't Tom's weight that had changed; *it was his relationship with the earth, his body, and everything around him that changed.* Tom repeated the process a number of times, much to the amazement of his two lifters. They later reported that if they hadn't experienced it, they wouldn't have believed it. In one second, their long-held ideas about what constituted power and strength were dramatically disproved.

Tom Crum is an expert in aikido. Many of the techniques that help us to learn how to center ourselves physically come from this martial art. Aikido talks of three major components of centering: ENERGY, THE BODY'S CENTER OF GRAVITY, and FLOW. They can be explained as follows:

ENERGY. In the martial arts, it is taught that we have within and around us a universal energy known as *ki* in Japan and *chi* in China. We can connect with this powerful energy any time we wish. When Tom made himself an immovable object to his two lifters, he was using his *chi* (energy) in combination with gravity and his connection to the earth to create extreme heaviness within the body. This is exactly what a child instinctively does to make himself unliftable when he doesn't want to be picked up to go to bed. Obviously his weight hasn't changed; somehow he intuitively knows how to use his *chi* to get his own way.

We are all familiar with stories of people lifting something as heavy as a car because a loved one is trapped underneath. Under normal circumstances they are not able to perform such a feat. But in an emergency this inner *chi* is there for the taking. Author and martial arts expert Chungliang Al Huang quips that . . .

"Human being is very small but chi-power is immense."[2]

All of this is good news. *To know that this kind of strength is available to us is very reassuring indeed!* It would make us feel even more confident if we learned how to access this power at will.

THE BODY'S CENTER OF GRAVITY. In the martial arts, the body's center of gravity is called the *dantien* (sometimes spelled *tantien* or *tai-ten*). Huang tells us that the literal meaning of *dantien* is "the field (or reservoir) of vital essence, the gut force in the belly."[3] All of the *chi*-power described above is held in the *dantien*, which is a spot about an inch and a half to three inches below the navel. When someone says "return to center" in the martial arts, that means focus your attention on the *dantien* and let your actions derive from this always available point of balance and power.

We ALL have this place within from which we can radiate immense power. Huang calls it the "fireplace." He teaches us that if you are feeling alive, blissful, and in tune with the world, your fireplace is working. If you are not feeling these wonderful things, it's time to stoke your fire!

FLOW. The immense power of flow will shock those who think the greatest power is in the fist. There is another aikido demonstration called "the unbendable arm." If someone of relatively equal strength tries to bend your outstretched arm by holding the biceps with one hand and pushing up your wrist with the other, you will do what we all were trained to do—tense up to resist the force. But he or she will most likely be able to bend your arm.

There is another way. Imagine your center (*dantien*) as an infinite source of water, your outstretched arm a fire hose, and your fingers the nozzle of the fire hose. Then in your mind's eye, turn on the water, imagining it coursing full force from your *dantien* through your shoulders through your outstretched fingers. Instead of tensing up and resisting the efforts to bend your arm, relax your shoulders and wiggle your fingers so that the water can flow in an unobstructed manner. Don't lock your arm; keep it slightly bent. Imagine the water gushing forward as far as the eye can see, through everything in its way, to infinity. Then, when you are totally focused on the strong flow of the water from your *dantien* to infinity, the person will find it impossible to bend your arm. *The flow of unlimited energy turns out to be much stronger than mere muscle fibers.*

Ultimately we learn that we can't be centered with a tense body (or with a limp body), only one that is allowing the powerful energy of the *dantien* to flow throughout our body into the external world. Now you understand what Tom Crum did to keep himself "unliftable"; he imagined the energy from his center or *dantien* flowing strongly through his legs and connecting deeply with the earth, thus creating a sense of rootedness and heaviness. Amazingly simple!

It is not wise to try these experiments without some coaching, so I suggest that you learn these physical demonstrations of aikido with the guidance of someone who is familiar with them. Or you may want to actually study with a martial arts expert.*

When we combine a centered mind with a centered body, the results are extraordinary. In the next chapter I describe a daily exercise derived from the martial arts that embodies all of the principles of centering, plus much more. It is an exercise that can be done by everyone—young or old, weak or strong—and its effect on our lives is magnificent.

To give you an incentive to investigate further this process of centering, let me describe some of the advantages of learning how to

---

*If you decide to study aikido or any of the martial arts, understand that some instructors stress only the aggressive aspects of the martial arts. Other instructors feel that the deepest purpose of the martial arts is to bring about a feeling of Spiritual aliveness, serenity, self-confidence, and centeredness. Obviously, for the purposes of ending the struggle and dancing with life, you want the latter.

create this dynamic alignment of body, mind, and Higher Self in our everyday lives.

Centering gives us a greater sense of safety. As my experience on the sailboat points out, centering not only makes us feel like an integrated whole—body, mind, and Higher Self—it also makes us feel a grand connection with the world around us.

I remember when I was working with the poor in New York, I often found myself on what were considered dangerous streets. Yet I never felt at risk. Looking back, I now realize that I was intuitively centering myself in a number of ways. I had a deep sense of caring for the people in the neighborhood. I did not see them as my enemies but as my friends. Hence, I was projecting an energy of love. I felt strong, relaxed, loving, and confident—the best way to walk any city streets. I walked tall and connected with the earth. Fearful people contract their energy, but mine was expanded. I believe that because of this centered state, I never had a moment of trouble befall me. It actually never occurred to me that I would!

Even though the streets everywhere have become a lot more dangerous since then, I believe that we are much safer when we are in a centered state. Those interested in doing harm would much prefer to approach the uncentered—the weak and scattered. If our energy says STRONG, people leave us alone; if our energy says WEAK, we are targets for those who are looking to do harm. I know that most police officers would agree with this assessment.

Centering makes us more intuitive. Centering is not a state of limpness; it is a state of immense clarity and focus. As a result, our awareness is heightened and our intuition is sharp. You really learn to "listen to" and "feel" the environment around you. This may explain why, when I was on the sailboat, I was able to find the lighthouse when John was floundering. In this heightened state of awareness, you somehow "know" where to go, what to do, what to say, and to whom. You also sense where *not* to go if danger is present. As a result, we learn to trust our intuition to show us the way.

Centering helps us feel fulfilled. When we are constantly focused on externals, we are not centered. In fact, we are pulled out of our center. We are not focusing on our real points of power and love. We are not aligned—body, mind, and Higher Self. Without that alignment, we always feel empty and lost, not comfortable within our being, and always trying to find our way Home. I've talked about this in my earlier books as a sense of Divine Homesickness.[4] From this place, we never feel fulfilled. We are always looking for something to fill us up. And nothing *out there* can.

When we are centered and, thus, feeling fulfilled, it doesn't matter what table we get, how heavy the traffic is, how the stock market rises and falls, and so on. The reason we get upset in those situations is that we are toppled over by externals. "If I had the right table, then I would feel happy." "If I made money in the stock market, then I would feel happy." What if you were already happy? Then it would all be all right! Nothing to get. Nothing to change. So one of the avenues for learning how to make "it all all right" as I talked about in Chapter 7 is to learn the art of centering. A big bonus indeed!

Centering gives us a sense of stability. If we leave our center and are continually reaching out to others to satisfy some lack within ourselves, we topple forward. If we constantly withdraw because of fear, we topple backward in a state of rigidity. If we are not rooted to the Universal energy within us, we will find ourselves tossing and tumbling all over the place, lacking any conviction, and latching on to anything that will appear to give us some stability. When we learn how to center, we are not affected as much by the ebb and flow of life. Our fear diminishes greatly. When things are not going according to plan in our outer life, we are positioned well to weather the storm.

Centering helps us resolve conflicts. Every day brings us conflict, whether it is with our children, our boss, the traffic, or whatever. When we get angry, we are not centered. When we are fearful, we are not centered. When people behave badly to us, they are not centered. Getting centered is the tool for dealing with conflict in our lives.

It is important to understand that, as I am using it, centering is not about going in for the attack. It is about creating an environment where attack is not necessary. In order to end the struggle and dance with life, we don't get stronger in order to conquer. We get stronger in order to be the very best that we can be.

When we are centered we are able to get in touch with a huge amount of power and love we hold inside. As we extend this caring energy from our *dantien* to any object of conflict, we are already creating a healing environment that says, "Let's make this work." We bring forward from within ourselves a sense of understanding, empathy, and trust. In this spirit of connectedness, we have a wonderful ability to resolve conflict.

Think about relationships. When our mate withdraws, we also have a tendency to withdraw in the hopes of protecting ourselves. If this pattern continues for a long time, we seem to disappear from each other's lives. If we can come forward, extending our loving *chi* instead of retracting it, I suspect there will be many more happier relationships around.

As an exercise, if anyone is acting hostilely toward you, silently project the words "I love you" while sending a warm healing light from your *dantien* onto his or her being. You may be surprised to find the person you are in conflict with changes his or her tune considerably. The hardest part of this exercise is keeping your energy positive when you are the subject of an attack. Not easy! But remember that everyone in our lives is a practice person, and when someone is throwing hostility your way, you have a perfect opportunity to practice projecting "I love you."

As we learn more about *chi, centering,* and *flow,* we learn that we can direct a positive ray of energy from our *dantien* to any person and place outside our body.

Centering helps us connect with others. Some people enter a room and seem to disappear into the crowd; their *chi* is contracted. Others loom with vibrancy; their *chi* is expanded. When we talk about a person having charisma, we are talking about his or her ability to radiate a magnetic energy, to extend the *chi.* Again, this is something that can be developed. People don't have to be wallflowers if they don't want to be. They can learn to extend their *chi* and be magnets to everyone in the room.

Chi has a lot to do with our emotional state. When we are feeling positive, light, happy, and loving, we are able to radiate a magnetic energy. When we enter a room, people notice us and want to be around us. When we are feeling negative, heavy, and gloomy, people do anything to avoid us. Who wants to be around all that negativity? Those who love punishment, I guess!

In *Dare to Connect*, I give you many tools for confidently and safely connecting with others. They are all tools that help us extend our *chi* in the most glorious way. For example, when entering that crowded room filled with strangers,

Stand tall as if your center were filled with an abundant supply of confidence and love.

Affirm to yourself that no matter what reaction you get, you are a worthwhile person who has much to give to this world. A very centering thought!

Focus on what you are going *to give* from your center of power and love, rather than on what you are going *to get* in the way of approval or acceptance from other people.

Walk into the room with an intention to make everyone feel great about themselves by radiating your loving energy from your center to everyone around you.

Can you see how this kind of approach would take away your fear and make you much more attractive to others? Contrast this to cowering in fear because you might not be liked or you are dressed inappropriately or you should have lost ten pounds or you have nothing to say to anyone. That kind of thinking sets up a stance of inferiority and an energy of weakness. Again, who would come running over to share your energy?

The great thing about learning to center is that it is an art that can be carried into all experiences. Also in *Dare to Connect*, I demonstrate how I use centering techniques to help me conquer any fear when I'm speaking to a large crowd of people.[5]

Before I approach the stage, I find a way of looking at the faces in my audience from wherever I am sitting or standing.

As I scan the audience, I extend my *chi* by *silently* repeating over and over again, "I love you. I love you. I love you. I love you." I know it sounds corny, but, believe me, as I do this my nervousness begins to melt away and I begin to feel a loving connection with the audience.

Once I am introduced, I walk up on the stage and I physically center myself, feeling my feet planted firmly on the ground with roots going down into the earth. As I do this I visualize myself aligned with my Higher Self and remind myself that my only purpose is to give love.

I then imagine a ray of light emerging from above, filling my being with light, flowing into the room, and surrounding everyone sitting before me. These last two steps sound rather time-consuming but take only a few seconds.

I cannot describe the high I get when I connect with my audience from that place of love and sharing. This is in contrast to those days when my knees knocked, my heart pounded, and I was petrified I wouldn't be "the best." When I speak in a centered way, I am rooted yet fluid, joyful, and totally connected with my audience.

Centering always makes us feel at Home. By staying centered, we see ourselves firmly rooted in our own Universe. This keeps us from always trying to attach ourselves to someone else's. It also is very transportable; we can take our center with us wherever we go, so how can we ever feel lost? Ram Dass tells the wonderful story of missing his home on one of his speaking tours around the country. One evening he walked into his hotel room and sat down, feeling lost and alone. He then reminded himself that he carries his Home everywhere he goes. Of course! At this revelation, he exited his room, closing the door behind him. He then turned around and re-opened the door, walked in, and yelled, "I'm home!" He didn't feel lost anymore. *We are always Home when we stay close to the center of our being.*

These are just a few ways that centering contributes to the quality of our lives. To enhance the process further, it is wise to create for ourselves a CENTERED ENVIRONMENT. (We need all the help we can get!) For example, it is very important that we develop friendships with positive people rather than "complaint buddies." People who are always complaining are not centered; by definition they are letting the world around them affect their happiness—and ours, if we allow it. When we are choosing centered friends, we are creating a more stable environment for ourselves. This, of course, helps us deal with those times when we find it necessary to be around people who are scattered and weak.

We can also center our home by surrounding ourselves with things that nourish us. For example, placing affirmations and insightful quotes where we can see them helps us focus on the beauty in our lives. Having welcoming colors on our walls and furniture creates a feeling of warmth. Objects that delight us help as well. The laughing Buddha on my desk always reminds me to come back to center.

I have seen so many people live in limbo environments. Some are waiting for a man or woman to come along and make their life complete. Some have separated from their mates and have never unpacked their boxes—literally and figuratively. They have lost one home but have not created another. Look around your own home and see what needs to be done to give you an environment of love and power. Then make the necessary changes.

There are many ways that we can incorporate the concept of centering into our everyday lives. I've given you just a brief sampling. I suggest you delve even more deeply into this fascinating tool. Again, it is important to create *daily practices* for aligning with the highest part of who we are. We don't get centered and stay there for the rest of our lives. In this chaotic world, it is so easy to be pulled out of our center. But it is very reassuring to know that we always have the tools to bring ourselves back into a place of power once again. We only have to *notice* when it's time to pull ourselves together again, and again, and again, and again.

There are *always* adjustments that have to be made in order to keep our sea legs in a constantly changing world. And a centered state definitely allows us to stay on course in a loving and powerful way. You can now understand why CENTERING is a magnificent tool for ending the struggle and dancing with life.

OVE INTO THE FLOW MOVE INTO THE FLOW MOVE INTO THE FLOW MOVE INTO THE FLOW
OVE INTO THE FLOW MOVE INTO THE FLOW MOVE INTO THE FLOW MOVE INTO THE FLOW
OVE INTO THE FLOW MOVE INTO THE FLOW MOVE INTO THE FLOW MOVE INTO THE FLOW
OVE INTO THE FLOW MOVE INTO THE FLOW MOVE INTO THE FLOW MOVE INTO THE FLOW
OVE INTO THE FLOW MOVE INTO THE FLOW MOVE INTO THE FLOW MOVE INTO THE FLOW
OVE INTO THE INTO THE FLOW
OVE INTO THE INTO THE FLOW
OVE INTO THE INTO THE FLOW
OVE INTO THE INTO THE FLOW
OVE INTO THE INTO THE FLOW

16

DANCE THE DANCE OF LIFE

OVE INTO THE FLOW MOVE INTO THE FLOW MOVE INTO THE FLOW MOVE INTO THE FLOW
OVE INTO THE FLOW MOVE INTO THE FLOW MOVE INTO THE FLOW MOVE INTO THE FLOW
OVE INTO THE FLOW MOVE INTO THE FLOW MOVE INTO THE FLOW MOVE INTO THE FLOW
OVE INTO THE FLOW MOVE INTO THE FLOW MOVE INTO THE FLOW MOVE INTO THE FLOW
OVE INTO THE FLOW MOVE INTO THE FLOW MOVE INTO THE FLOW MOVE INTO THE FLOW
OVE INTO THE FLOW MOVE INTO THE FLOW MOVE INTO THE FLOW MOVE INTO THE FLOW
OVE INTO THE FLOW MOVE INTO THE FLOW MOVE INTO THE FLOW MOVE INTO THE FLOW
OVE INTO THE FLOW MOVE INTO THE FLOW MOVE INTO THE FLOW MOVE INTO THE FLOW
OVE INTO THE FLOW MOVE INTO THE FLOW MOVE INTO THE FLOW MOVE INTO THE FLOW
OVE INTO THE FLOW MOVE INTO THE FLOW MOVE INTO THE FLOW MOVE INTO THE FLOW
OVE INTO THE FLOW MOVE INTO THE FLOW MOVE INTO THE FLOW MOVE INTO THE FLOW
OVE INTO THE FLOW MOVE INTO THE FLOW MOVE INTO THE FLOW MOVE INTO THE FLOW
OVE INTO THE FLOW MOVE INTO THE FLOW MOVE INTO THE FLOW MOVE INTO THE FLOW
OVE INTO THE FLOW MOVE INTO THE FLOW MOVE INTO THE FLOW MOVE INTO THE FLOW
OVE INTO THE FLOW MOVE INTO THE FLOW MOVE INTO THE FLOW MOVE INTO THE FLOW
OVE INTO THE FLOW MOVE INTO THE FLOW MOVE INTO THE FLOW MOVE INTO THE FLOW
OVE INTO THE FLOW MOVE INTO THE FLOW MOVE INTO THE FLOW MOVE INTO THE FLOW
OVE INTO THE FLOW MOVE INTO THE FLOW MOVE INTO THE FLOW MOVE INTO THE FLOW
OVE INTO THE FLOW MOVE INTO THE FLOW MOVE INTO THE FLOW MOVE INTO THE FLOW
OVE INTO THE FLOW MOVE INTO THE FLOW MOVE INTO THE FLOW MOVE INTO THE FLOW

> *The same stream of life that runs through the world runs through my veins night and day and dances in rhythmic measure. It is the same life that shoots in joy through the dust of the earth into numberless blades of grass and breaks into tumultuous waves of leaves and flowers.*
>
> Rabindranath Tagore[1]

IT WAS A BEAUTIFUL DAY. THE SUN was pouring into my window as I awoke in my hotel room in San Francisco. I got out of bed and went to the window to look at the wonderful view. There, something out of the ordinary caught my attention. In the park across the street, I noticed many Chinese men and women of all ages doing a graceful, peaceful, meditative dance. Some were dressed very casually and others were in suits obviously on their way to work.

I was mesmerized by the sweetness of the slow, fluid, seemingly purposeful movements. You have to understand that I am a person who is repelled by anything that looks like exercise! But this set of movements was totally drawing me in, and I had to learn what it was all about.

Upon inquiry I discovered that the flowing movements I had witnessed were a form of the martial arts called TAI CHI (also spelled TAI JI), which comes from the teachings of the Tao. I have seen many different definitions of tai chi and they are all in harmony with the idea of moving effortlessly and freely with the flow of nature. What a perfect dance in today's times of struggle! I also learned that dancing tai chi in the park was not a phenomenon only in San Francisco. Millions of people in China practice tai chi, usually in groups, every morning before work.

There are many forms of tai chi. It can be studied as a strict discipline with exact positions and years of study. Or it can be simply enjoyed as a moving meditation or dance that helps to center us, thus keeping us focused on our power, our love, and our connection to all things. For the purposes of ending the struggle, the latter is definitely preferable.

My frustration in writing this chapter is that I am not able to pull you over to that hotel window in San Francisco and say, "Wow! Look at this!" Nor am I able to pull you out of your chair and say, "Come on! Do this with me! See how wonderful it feels!" The written word does have its limitations. But let me suggest that you order a very beautiful videotape featuring Nikki Winston, which will allow you not only to take in the inherent beauty of tai chi but also *immediately to learn how to do it.*[2]

Winston demonstrates fourteen very simple yet meaningful movements from which you can absorb the magic and majesty of the dance. You will find that the movement and the music combined with the life-altering metaphors that Winston presents are transformative indeed. I have made it a morning ritual to take twenty minutes and dance tai chi with her à la her videotape. *What a wonderful way to start the day!* I believe that when you are introduced to the magical movements and metaphors of tai chi you will also want to make it a daily ritual, your reminder of all that is beautiful in this world.[3]

Understand that *you do not have to be a great dancer to study tai chi.* Even if you have the proverbial two left feet, it will work beautifully for you. Tai chi can be practiced by strapping athletes and by feeble senior citizens. Even those confined to a wheelchair can derive enormous benefits from adopting these movements and metaphors into their everyday lives.

One of the most noticeable features of tai chi is its hypnotically slow pace. It is as though you are seeing it through the lens of a slow-motion camera. And when you dance tai chi, it is as though your world is slowing down in an incredibly peaceful way and allowing you to look mindfully and deeply at everything you see. Each step rolls into the next with a beautiful sense of fluidity. Just the slow pace gives one a feeling of serenity and awe. Tai chi isn't about trying harder; it's about "trying softer." It's about living your life with flow instead of force.

Not only is there a feeling of peace in the actual movements of tai chi, but *the profound meaning of each movement satisfies a deep yearning within our being.* When both are combined, the benefits that are attributed to tai chi are enormous. To name a few:

> Tai chi helps us focus on the present, relieves stress, increases our ability to appreciate all the gifts in our lives, makes us feel more secure knowing there are many supports within and around us, helps us slow the aging process, helps circulation, helps us feel centered, grounded, relaxed, alert, aware, and energized—and it helps the Spirit soar!

I repeat, not a bad way to start the day.

Why does tai chi have such an amazing effect? In the first place, tai chi takes all its movements and metaphors from nature. Those who created it many millennia ago believed that *if you want to understand and appreciate life, watch nature.* You may be asking (especially if you are living in a major city), "In this day and age, what could nature possibly have to contribute to my everyday life?" Plenty! Nature gives us many models for "right living." The "five elements" used in the tai chi dance are a perfect example:[4]

> **FIRE.** The element of fire is about letting our inner light shine through. It represents being alive and being in love with life. It is about the gifts we have to give to this world. Everyone possesses the gift of fire, but too many of us hold back, afraid we may turn people off with our power. With tai

chi, we learn how beautiful it is to shine our light into this world and not to hold back.

WATER. The coolness of water complements the heat of the fire within us. Fire is described as the yang or male element; water is described as the yin or female element—a perfect balancing act. Yet while water is described as gentle and easy, it also has its own kind of power. Remember that rocks are worn away by water.

We can learn a lot by watching how water relates to the world around it. It's fluid. It goes around any obstacle in its way. (It doesn't stop to argue!) It flows downstream rather than struggling to push upstream as many of us are doing in life. It just goes with the flow. Perhaps that's why watching the action and rhythm of water is so peaceful to the human psyche. It demonstrates a way of being that we all yearn to embrace.

WOOD. A tree is strong and rooted yet very flexible. It reaches up to the sky and sinks down into the ground to receive its nourishment. A tree "sees" in all directions. It suggests that we take the time really to look around and be open to new experiences. No two trees are alike, yet they are all beautiful and, as they sway with the movement of the wind, they all do their own dance. A beautiful lesson for us humans to learn!

METAL. Gold is often the symbol for the metal element. It represents everything in the outside world that would contribute to our highest good. Tai chi teaches us that we have the power to bring into our world all that we need and that there are never any shortages of love, nourishment, and riches out there.

EARTH. The earth represents what is stable. When we connect with the earth, we feel powerful and rooted. As I pointed out in the last chapter, when Tom Crum became "unliftable," he connected with the earth element. He directed the *chi* from his *dantien* through his feet and into the ground. Like a tree, it was very difficult to uproot him. When we plant our energy into the earth, it is very difficult to uproot us as well.

Using symbols from nature, tai chi teaches us how to balance the yin and the yang energies (the female and male energies) within our being. The wisdom of the ages tells us that . . .

"Yang is fire in nature. Too much fire, and you will burn the herbs. Yin is water in nature. Too much water, and the herbs will rot."[5]

Indeed! Too much of a good thing can be damaging. We definitely need balance in terms of our male and female roles. The ancient wisdom from which tai chi was derived would never have agreed that men should be only yang (strong, active, and aggressive) and women only yin (passive, yielding, nurturing). This is creating an imbalance. We must integrate both into our being. And then we will know harmony.

We also need balance in our everyday world. This balance is often difficult to achieve in the middle of the multitude of things happening around us—children crying, traffic roaring, televisions blaring, bosses yelling, work piling up. Can you see how turning to the symbolism in nature for just a few minutes can bring a sense of calm in the middle of a hectic day?

There are other symbolisms in the tai chi dance that help us achieve a balanced life. Let me demonstrate by giving you the profound meanings inherent in the fourteen movements that Winston provides for us in her excellent tai chi video.

1. First, you always need to step back and take a look inside before venturing out into the world. Reflection is good for the body, mind, and Soul. It helps you discover the essence of who you are and your connection to all

things. It also helps you notice where you are stuck in your Journey through life and what steps you need to take to get yourself moving forward once again.

2. It's then time to open up to life. Part the beaded curtain that keeps you from seeing all that you can see. As you open up into the light, you expand your perspective and realize the huge amount of resources that are there for the taking.

3. You reach up to the sky and down to the earth and bring the energy of the Universe into every cell of your being. The sky represents your dreams, and the earth, your reality. Integrate them both into your being, bringing balance into your vision. The potential is unlimited. Feel yourself standing tall, centered, and strong. You are never without the powerful resources of the Universe.

4. As you pull in all the energy you need from the earth and sky, you place it in the *dantien*, the center of your being, and fuel the fire that is your creative energy. Feel it fill your entire being.

5. Then spread your fire into the world. Don't hold back. Give the gift of who you are to everyone around you. Make your essence warm this world as far as the eye can see. Visualize those who receive your powerful spark of life being nourished by your gift. Feel the passion and the beauty of being alive.

6. Balance your energy by letting a gentle stream of water pour over and through you, clearing any areas in your life that are blocked. Let the water cool you and keep you from being consumed by the fire. Allow yourself to

feel totally relaxed and fluid as the water finds its way into the earth below you.

7. Like a tree, plant yourself firmly in the ground, allowing your branches to sway with the wind, flexible and unbreakable. Stand tall, feeling the warmth of the sun nourish your entire being. Take a look around. See the abundance of opportunities that surrounds you.

8. Now choose the "gold" you would like to bring into your world. Gather up what you need to sustain you—love, strength, connection, or whatever riches you want in your life. Bring it all into your heart and into your center. Feel the abundance in your life. Love it. Enjoy it.

9. And then let go. Don't become attached to anything in your life. As you understand the essence of who you are and your connection with all things, you learn that you never have to hold on to *anything*. You can love it all, enjoy it all, but you need not hang on. There is always more. As you let go of all the fear and suffering that attachment brings, you are free. Feel the relief this freedom brings. Feel yourself lighten from all the unnecessary burdens your attachments have created in your life.

10. Feeling free, you can fly like an eagle, which is sometimes called the bird of enlightenment. An old Native American tale tells us to put our prayers on the wings of eagles as they are the birds that can fly closest to the sun, closest to God. Feeling light and free, you are able to soar. You are able to feel the freedom of an unencumbered life.

11. With that sense of freedom, return to earth. Let yourself feel grounded and whole. Feel the strength of the sky above your head and the earth below your feet, and let them both nourish your Spirit.

12. As you pull the energy from the earth into and throughout your entire body, let yourself open like a golden lotus, which symbolizes the wisdom and beauty that is your essence. Let the joy of unfolding into a beautiful flower permeate your being and spill over into the world around you. A joyful sight indeed!

13. Then "embrace tiger," which means embrace all of life. Accept and welcome it all. Don't push any of it away. Embrace who you are. Embrace the challenges. Embrace your fears. Embrace your joys. Embrace your weaknesses. Embrace your strength. Embrace being alive. Embrace all that is.

14. Finally, "return to mountain." Return to center. Return Home. You are safe. You are grounded. You are whole. You are free. You are on solid ground. Honor the moment and the place you now are in. Honor your feelings. Honor your Journey in life thus far. This is *your* mountaintop. Embrace it and be at peace.

Fourteen steps of an incredible journey! As you can see, this simple dance of tai chi encompasses the essence of everything I have written about in this book thus far—releasing, embracing, meditating, being joyful, being peaceful, being mindful, being balanced, creating rituals, giving thanks, slowing down, centering, knowing that all is well, transcending the petty, climbing the ladder to true success, feeling safe, having patience, flowing with the Universe, and more.

As you begin each day with a number of repetitions of these movements, you can't help but walk the earth in a more powerful and loving way. And through *daily* repetition, you being to alter your relationship to everything around you. *Know that every time you "return to mountain," you return a new person.* You come back with deeper consciousness of what is inherently your essence. You understand better that life is a constant opening and closing, giving and receiving, flowing yet staying rooted. You begin peeling off the layers of conditioning that keep you trapped in a rigid, linear way of thinking. Each time you return home, everything begins anew.

I can't stress enough how powerful it is to combine the bodily movements with the symbolism inherent in tai chi. The effect is magnified enormously. For example, each time I "let go" by releasing my arms and spreading them wide (Step 9), I find myself taking a deep breath of relief. Sometimes I am moved to tears. Letting go is obviously an area that I struggle with in some areas of my life. And to be able to let go is a blessing indeed.

Each time I repeat this movement, knowing what it means, I let go of a little bit more and more and more. As I keep releasing, I feel myself getting lighter and lighter. The words "let go" on their own are powerful; but when combined with the physical act that represents letting go, I am touched even more deeply. Sometimes I linger on this one movement over and over again just to feel the relief this simple act brings to me. And sometimes in the middle of the day, when I know I am causing myself upset because I am holding on to something much too tightly, I will actually get up and repeat the movement associated with Step 9 and take a deep breath. Instant relief! Even if I do this physical movement in my mind's eye, I feel myself lighten.

Naturally tai chi on the top of a mountain is sublime. But strangely, when I do my little tai chi dance in the course of a very busy day, it has even more impact. Being on top of a mountain is already being out of the everyday petty. But it's when we're in the middle of the petty that we need something to help us remember the essence of who we are.

So when you feel yourself pulled far from your center in the middle of a busy day, tai chi helps you find your center once again. It's so easy simply to stand up and perform the tai chi movements a few times. It's amazing how good you will feel. I see it as taking a vacation in the middle of a hectic day.

With constant repetition, we begin to live into the meaning of each of these metaphors and movements, and as a result our relationship to everything around us is altered. So I urge you to obtain the videotape I suggested as a good beginning. In addition, you may want to enroll in a workshop or an ongoing tai chi class if there is one in your area.

A word about tai chi instructors: Understand that different teachers have different metaphors and movements. This is a plus since the more input you have, the richer tai chi will seem to you. On the negative side, some tai chi teachers just try to teach only the movements. This is unfortunate, since the metaphors give so much meaning to the movements. For the purposes of ending the struggle and dancing with life, you want a teacher who provides both, which is sometimes hard to find.

You also want a teacher who wants you to dance your own dance. Many are into teaching exact form. Again, for the purposes of ending the struggle and dancing with life, this is not what you want. When we are going for perfection, we are only perpetuating our rigidity, our need to control all those things that create struggle in our lives. Remember:

We weren't born to hold on to positions. Nor are we meant to be perfect. We are meant to flow in a world that is constantly moving beneath our feet.

Sometimes people who get locked into certain tai chi styles get judgmental about others. There is nothing fluid about righteousness! We all love things beautifully packaged in our society, but that's not what tai chi is all about.

There is the popular story of a tai chi master whose disciples had a beautiful flow except when they moved to the right side; there, they had a strange dip. People would ask the disciples, "Why do you do it that way?" They would answer, "That's the way my master did it." What the disciples didn't take into account was that the master had one leg shorter than the other. If they had been respecting their own essence and not imitating their master, they certainly wouldn't have done it that way!

You know that you are in a good class or have purchased the right videotape if your teacher makes you feel great about yourself and awakens the Spiritual part of who you are. As I see it, the primary job of any teacher is to give you the space to discover more about yourself, to discover your own tai chi.

Yes, everyone has his or her own dance to dance, literally and figuratively. Some of us want to spread our arms wide to new adventures. Some of us want to open the curtain just a little bit for the time being. Some of us want to light a huge bonfire. Some of us want just a little flame to radiate our own special light into the world. Never worry if you are doing it wrong. There is no wrong. It's your dance. And every day it's a new dance for all of us. It is important to trust your own rhythm, your own movement.

Initially we may feel a little awkward trying to learn the movements. But in a *very* short time we begin to feel a sense of ease and flow. And as our own essence emerges, we feel a wonderful sense of freedom, expansion, security, and peace. In a world of constant change, we need daily reminders that all is well. And when we dance the dance of tai chi, we know that ALL *IS* WELL!

As I said earlier, tai chi has been called a "moving meditation," and as such it is sublime. It quiets the mind and focuses us on the Spiritual aspect of life from which we draw our power, our sense of flow, our joy. There are many who feel that a moving meditation gives a greater sense of tranquility than a sitting meditation. This is especially true if you have difficulty sitting still. If this is the case for you, tai chi can ease your way into meditation. Others believe that since our life is one of motion, a moving meditation translates better into the everyday world. And they prefer the moving meditation of tai chi.

Tai chi is not only a moving meditation. *It is also a powerful set of affirmations translated in the body.* These affirmations tell us . . .

I am free. I am fluid. I am connected. I am rich. I am whole. I embrace it all. I am nourished. I have much to give. I can soar. I am at peace. I let go.

Affirmations work best when we are able to store their messages within our body. The affirmations of tai chi establish an energy of power in and around us. We don't have to accept the negativity of the chatter in our mind. We can show it another way.

The key is to keep practicing tai chi until it inserts itself into our everyday lives, until we can say to ourselves, *"I live my life in a tai chi way."* To me,

Living in a tai chi way means . . . functioning naturally and smoothly . . . in an uncluttered way . . . totally in tune with the Universe . . . with all our expectations and clinging dropping to the wayside . . . as we learn the secret of flowing with all that happens around us.

That's a tall order but something definitely worth working toward. Obviously tai chi doesn't change the outside world. What it does do is teach us how to stay centered in the midst of any turmoil surrounding us. It gives us our sea legs. It also helps us return Home when we have lost our way. When we have that stillness in the depths of our being, we have a haven to which we can *always* return. And what's best about it is that it's a portable haven. We can take it with us wherever we go.

So give yourself the gift of tai chi. If you have children, include them in the practice of this beautiful dance. How wonderful for them to learn at an early age the life-affirming lessons it can teach them. Young or old, I think we ALL need to join the millions of Chinese who begin their day with tai chi. As we harmonize our body, mind, and Higher Self at the beginning of each day, we walk the world in a totally powerful and loving way. What a gift to ourselves and to the world around us!

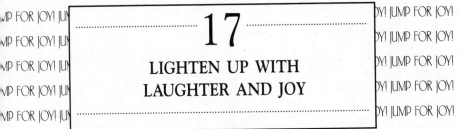

17

LIGHTEN UP WITH
LAUGHTER AND JOY

ET ME ASK YOU SOMETHING.
When's the last time you can remember walking around with a smile
on your face, a laugh in your belly, lightness in your heart, and a
sense of exuberance at the sheer wonder of being alive?

That long ago, huh? Well, you're not alone. It seems that we
live in a very "heavy" world at the present moment. There is so
much that seems to be weighing us down. Lightness and fun are
missing elements in most people's lives.

It is very telling that workshops are now being conducted that
teach people how to laugh and have fun![2] This says something very
poignant about our society. It says that we have lost our ability to
appreciate three of the greatest gifts we have been given—lightness,
laughter, and joy.

Just look around. Business is *so* serious. Sports are *so* serious. Relationships are *so* serious. Parenting is *so* serious. Even sexuality and
food, potentially two of the most joyous gifts we have been given,
have become *so* serious. We've lost our ability truly to enjoy.

Aside from our intense seriousness, we are such a rational, logical, methodical, and structured society. How can we ever learn to
dance with life when we are so uptight? Dancing with life by definition means curving, blending, bending, circling, and flowing—like

nature. "Bad" dancers are straight, stiff, and methodical, totally out of harmony with the ceaseless flow of the energy of the Universe.

Jungian analyst Robert Johnson has a name for this ceaseless flow of energy. He calls it the "dionysian energy." And he describes it as "the power of life that flows through all of us and unites us with heaven and earth."[3] A beautiful image indeed! Dionysus was the Greek god of wine and ecstasy, and although this popular Greek god is sometimes characterized in a negative light, Johnson describes his positive image. He says that we are touching the dionysian energy when we feel an invigorating energy charging throughout our bodies, just the kind of energy that makes us jump for joy.

Johnson makes a very important observation about what is happening in the world today. He says that when we don't allow the natural healthy dionysian quality within our being to emerge, we compensate by going for thrills any way we can get them, which could partly explain our addictions to drugs, alcohol, food, crime, violence, and rampant sex. These negative addictions can be seen as *dionysian energy gone awry.* They fill the void created by our loss of contact with the inherent sense of joy we hold inside. Johnson calls addiction "the negative side of Spiritual seeking." He says:

> "We are looking for an exultation of the spirit; but instead of fulfillment we get a short-lived physical thrill that can never satisfy the chronic, gnawing emptiness with which we are beset."[4]

If Johnson is correct, his conclusion says so much about what has gone awry in our society today. It says that . . .

So many of our addictions come from our inability to reach deep inside our being where the source of our joy resides and bring this joy into the dance of our everyday lives. In desperation we seek out temporary fixes anywhere we can find them, even if they result in our self-destruction.

So what is the answer? How do we bring back the twinkle in our eye that comes from the radiant light of our inner joy, our dionysian energy? Clearly, first and foremost, *we need to learn how to LIGHTEN UP!* As G. K. Chesterton reminds us, "Angels fly because they take themselves lightly!" Heaviness dims the light! All that I've spoken about so far has been about lightening up and finding the joy. Let me give you a few more pointers about finding the dionysian energy within.

PLANT A SMILE ON YOUR FACE. Don't ever underestimate the power of a smile. A smile is an instant "lightener." It can change all manner of things. And it is so easy to create. Thich Nhat Hanh, a renowned Zen monk, tells us to recite the following four lines silently as we breathe in and out:

"Breathing in, I calm my body.
Breathing out, I smile.
Dwelling in the present moment,
I know this is a wonderful moment!"[5]

A smile helps us know many things. It helps us know that even if we are sad about something, we are more than our sadness. It helps us know that we have the power to handle the many stresses we encounter. It helps us know we have much to be grateful for. A smile is a wonderful aid in helping us say YES to life.

So we can begin the process of lightening up and bringing joy into our lives with a simple smile. Smile when you are feeling troubled. Smile as you walk down the street. Smile when you awaken each morning. Smile when you meditate or do tai chi or say your affirmations. Smile when you look in that mirror. (Remember, *real* beauty comes from that smile.) Smile right now. How does it feel? Lighter? Happier? Oh, yes!

LEARN THE ART OF CREATING A REAL BELLY LAUGH.
It's easy to create a smile but much harder to create a laugh. But create it we must! Why?

Laughter is very healthy. It changes our internal chemistry from negative to positive.

Laughter gives us an internal massage, reaching many organs of the body.

Laughter is an amazing exercise: It tightens the belly.

Laughter releases tension.

Laughter makes life wonderful.

Laughter balances the heavy with lightness.

Laughter is contagious.

Laughter brightens up the world!

I find it interesting that we humans take ourselves so seriously when the human condition is actually quite humorous. We need to learn to laugh at ourselves with feelings of deep love, similar to parents laughing at the fumblings of children as they learn to walk.

We're all learning how to walk, and sometimes we walk into walls!

As with a smile, laughter needs to be part of our regular routine. Barry Stevens tells us that when she wakes up in the morning, she stretches, then she laughs.

"At first the laughter is artificial but soon it becomes ridiculous and then it becomes real laughter."[6]

Chungliang Al Huang, our tai chi master, is also a master at laughter. In his wonderfully entertaining book *Quantum Soup: Fortune Cookies in Crisis*, he tells us that "one of the most recommended Taoist and Zen meditations is to let your hair down, stick out your belly, and roar with laughter." And he tells us:

"To grow a proper laugh, start with the image of a baby (bamboo) shoot pushing up through the earth. Start with just the thoughts of laughter. Don't hurry it. Let it grow like the shoot. Wait for a genuine smile. Let it widen as a sound begins to tickle in the throat. Now let it begin to bounce around in the chest. Still, do not hurry it! Think now of the rapidly growing bamboo, rising to the sun, leaves atremble in the fresh spring air. Allow your body to follow the leaves, expanding in all directions. Your breath is bigger, deeper, wider. S-t-r-e-t-c-h-i-n-g. Let it grow. Watch it go. **Now** give it it's sound! A chuckle shakes the shoulders; a guffaw is born in the belly. **Haw—haw—haw—haw!** How it escapes through the mouth and quakes and shakes and blooms and booms. Your very fingers are atingle with it. Your toes and kneecaps and hips and lips become the very sound of laughter. It is everywhere. Haw—haw—haw! ('Is that me?' you think, and laugh ever more fully and freely at the absurdity of the thought.)"[7]

How wonderful! Huang also gives us much insight into the nature of joy and laughter at one of his tai chi workshops.[8] Here he shows us how really to make the belly jiggle and tells us that Confucius said not to trust someone who laughs without his or her belly heaving! So, he says, "Be generous with our gut!"

Another bit of helpful advice comes from Annette Goodheart, whose work specializes on laughter.

"Fake it 'til you make it. Fake the laughter until it really begins to happen. This works because the diaphragm is stupid—it can't tell if you are faking or not."[9]

You don't even need a reason to laugh. In fact, things can be going badly in your life and you can still laugh. As Goodheart further tells us,

"If you're going to be miserable, you might as well enjoy it!"[10]

My sister Marcia and I have mastered the art of using laughter to turn something painful into something light. Over the years, our laughter certainly has helped us "enjoy our misery." Even today, when one of us calls the other upset about something in life, we end up laughing ourselves silly. It's not that what we're upset about isn't important and doesn't have to be dealt with, but . . .

Humor creates a shift in perception that allows us to center ourselves in a powerful place.

The laughter helps us lighten up and detach from the drama, which allows us to see the more important larger picture, which is filled with many blessings. It balances the heaviness of the pain we are feeling with the lightness that comes from humor. And balance is what creates a world devoid of struggle. As long as we're not laughing at anyone's expense, laughter is, indeed, a gift for which to be grateful.

So bring laughter in all parts of your life, even as you go off to sleep. My husband and I used to watch the news before going to bed, but no more. Now we watch only comedy shows. Sleep is much better (and funnier) that way!

LEARN THE ART OF JUMPING FOR JOY. Many of us have not jumped for joy (literally or figuratively) in a very long time. The reason, as I pointed out in earlier chapters, is that we take so many things for granted. As you incorporate more tools of appreciation into your life, jumping for joy will become a regular occurrence. We must remember to celebrate every inner or outer "win" in our lives. I guess the greatest win of all is simply waking up every morning to the privilege of being alive. That's cause enough for jumping for joy. We don't have to wait for a big win in the external world.

Strangely, most of us don't even jump for joy when we have those wins in the external world. I speak from experience on that one. At one time, it was a dream of mine to have a book published. I truly jumped for joy the day I received a copy of my first published book in the mail. As time went on, many other of my books were published, some in as many as nineteen countries. This made two large shelves of my published works. But soon I took it all for granted. As each new edition of the books would come in the mail, I would mindlessly add it to the collection on my shelves without a moment of gratitude, without a moment of celebration.

One day, as I sat at my desk, I looked over at the bookshelf and the miracle of it all hit me. I stopped what I was doing, walked over to the bookshelf, and celebrated all those neglected successes for the very first time by jumping up and down for joy. I pulled out each book and thanked that particular publisher. I thanked the people who bought the books. I thanked myself for pushing through the fear and writing the books. I thanked my Higher Power for giving me the life force to be a part of this amazing world.

Most of us don't spend enough time appreciating our wins, big or small. We focus on what we haven't done or what needs to be done. *This by definition is choosing struggle instead of joy.* Keep this in mind as the next win comes into your life. Remember that true success comes from the noticing and the celebration of all our blessings.

BECOME HIGH ON LIFE. Beyond jumping for joy is something the Indian Vedas called *ananda*, which means bliss or inner joy. Bliss doesn't have to be exhibited externally, although it can be. It is something that radiates throughout and beyond our being.

I remind you of Sheila Byrd's letter in Chapter 5. She said "I lead a very simple life. Yet some nights I cannot sleep because I am so excited about the next day. I find joy and laughter in everything I do." Sheila Byrd is not a party animal; she doesn't do drugs; she doesn't need external stimuli to make her high. *She is high on life.* She experiences *ananda*. She draws all her joy and laughter from within, despite the fact that her life has been—and continues to be—very difficult.

Yes, even in the midst of very challenging circumstances we can learn how to turn our inner dial to joy instead of misery as Barry Neil Kaufman shows us in his moving book *Happiness Is a Choice*. Kaufman speaks of his and his wife's personal experience of totally healing their neurologically impaired and dysfunctioning child. When this potentially devastating circumstance first came into their life, they actively *chose* happiness instead of misery. And it made all the difference in the world. It is interesting that someone who also had a dysfunctioning child bitterly chastised Kaufman for taking something that was terrible and making believe it was beautiful. Kaufman gently replied,

"Did you ever consider that you might be taking something that's beautiful and making believe it's terrible?"[11]

Wow! A lesson for us all! Yes, happiness *is* a choice. We can find much to be joyous about in any situation in our life simply by turning our inner dial to joy.

Let me give you another example. Most people experience funerals as a time of tragedy. The dial in most people's hearts is set to misery and loss. But it doesn't have to be that way. I've been to funerals where the dial has been set to joy. This was the case when Diana, a dear friend of mine, lost her husband of twenty-five years. This was an intensely close marriage of two people working, playing, and creating together. She was the type of person who understood the principle that joy can be found in all things. Because of this she was able to create a funeral that celebrated, not mourned, her husband's life.

Many present at the funeral sat there with the mask of gloom and doom upon their faces. At one point Diana got up and asked her many friends who filled the church to get up and share humorous stories about her husband. Soon the church was filled with laughter and joy. As we exited the church, we were all handed a brightly colored balloon. We gathered in the churchyard and in unison released our balloons into the air, a symbolic gesture of sending her husband off with color and fanfare to the next stage of his Journey. And while he will be missed by all those who knew him, he will also be celebrated for all the beauty and laughter he brought into this world. What greater tribute is there than that.

It is important to mention that Diana did not avoid the Land of Tears. Before and after the funeral she mourned her heartfelt loss. But she did so not as a victim but with a deep appreciation of the twenty-five years they had together and an inner knowing that she would reach the other side of her pain—which, of course, she did. She is now very happily married once again, knowing in her heart that her husband kept his promise before he died—that he would send her someone wonderful to love. Heaven on earth is bringing *ananda* into our lives no matter what is happening externally.

In all my books and tapes I've talked about the Spiritual Journey. Let me emphasize that nowhere is it written that the Spiritual Journey has to be somber and joyless. In fact, the one characteristic that I have found to be universally present in highly Spiritual people is their enchanting sense of humor. They have learned the wisdom of laughter and lightness.

I recently heard an interview with a Spiritual leader. Throughout the interview he giggled and laughed and had a grand old time. At first he seemed a bit ridiculous, but in a short time, he had me giggling and laughing with him. The poor interviewer, who was of the dour and somber type, didn't know what to do with all this happiness and levity. As time went on, the interviewer was the one who seemed a bit ridiculous! One could *feel* the lightness of the Spiritual master and the heaviness of the interviewer. How different their experience of life must be!

I think if we were asked if there were any regrets as we reached the later stages of our lives, most of us would answer, "My biggest regret is that I didn't enjoy life more." I was very moved by the now popular statement attributed to an eighty-five-year-old woman named Nadine Starr:

> "If I had my life to live over, I would start barefoot earlier in the spring and stay that way later in the fall. I would go to more dances. I would ride more merry-go-rounds. I would pick more daisies."

What would you do differently if you had your life to live over again? Even if you are very young, this question has great relevance.

I suspect that you, like Nadine Starr, would choose to play more, appreciate more, and giggle more. Why not begin this very moment?

In *Opening Our Hearts to Men*,[12] I talked about the importance of creating a Higher-Life purpose, a reason for living that supersedes all other reasons. A Higher-Life purpose transcends all the Lower-Self purposes that have to do with the acquisition of externals, such as money, children, a relationship, a sexy body, owning a home and car, and so on. Although these can all bring us pleasure, they don't fill the inner void created by a lack of Higher-Self purpose.

Three of the Higher-Self purposes that I have created for myself at various times over the years are . . .

To learn and teach about love.
To open my heart.
To focus on giving instead of getting.

I have now created a new Higher-Self purpose for myself with the hope it will govern my life for many years to come. It is . . .

To let go, lighten up, laugh more, play more, and fully embrace my experiences of life.

Maybe in the long run our only purpose in life is to love and enjoy one another and dance (Spiritually speaking) the days and nights away.

I have come to believe that enjoyment of life is truly a gift from the Gods and is something that we are *obliged* to embrace with arms open wide. After all, the Gods would be insulted if we didn't! So smile, laugh, and jump for joy. Set your dial to happiness and watch the delicious energy of bliss radiate throughout your being into the entire world around you.

ONE STEP AT A TIME ONE STEP AT A TIME ONE STEP AT A TIME ONE STEP AT A TIME ONE STEP AT A TIME
ONE STEP AT A TIME ONE STEP AT A TIME ONE STEP AT A TIME ONE STEP AT A TIME ONE STEP AT A TIME
ONE STEP AT A TIME ONE STEP AT A TIME ONE STEP AT A TIME ONE STEP AT A TIME ONE STEP AT A TIME
ONE STEP AT A TIME ONE STEP AT A TIME ONE STEP AT A TIME ONE STEP AT A TIME ONE STEP AT A TIME
ONE STEP AT A TIME ONE STEP AT A TIME ONE STEP AT A TIME ONE STEP AT A TIME ONE STEP AT A TIME

18

TRUST THE GRAND DESIGN

ONE STEP AT A TIME ONE STEP AT A TIME ONE STEP AT A TIME ONE STEP AT A TIME ONE STEP AT A TIME
ONE STEP AT A TIME ONE STEP AT A TIME ONE STEP AT A TIME ONE STEP AT A TIME ONE STEP AT A TIME
ONE STEP AT A TIME ONE STEP AT A TIME ONE STEP AT A TIME ONE STEP AT A TIME ONE STEP AT A TIME
ONE STEP AT A TIME ONE STEP AT A TIME ONE STEP AT A TIME ONE STEP AT A TIME ONE STEP AT A TIME
ONE STEP AT A TIME ONE STEP AT A TIME ONE STEP AT A TIME ONE STEP AT A TIME ONE STEP AT A TIME
ONE STEP AT A TIME ONE STEP AT A TIME ONE STEP AT A TIME ONE STEP AT A TIME ONE STEP AT A TIME
ONE STEP AT A TIME ONE STEP AT A TIME ONE STEP AT A TIME ONE STEP AT A TIME ONE STEP AT A TIME
ONE STEP AT A TIME ONE STEP AT A TIME ONE STEP AT A TIME ONE STEP AT A TIME ONE STEP AT A TIME
ONE STEP AT A TIME ONE STEP AT A TIME ONE STEP AT A TIME ONE STEP AT A TIME ONE STEP AT A TIME
ONE STEP AT A TIME ONE STEP AT A TIME ONE STEP AT A TIME ONE STEP AT A TIME ONE STEP AT A TIME
ONE STEP AT A TIME ONE STEP AT A TIME ONE STEP AT A TIME ONE STEP AT A TIME ONE STEP AT A TIME
ONE STEP AT A TIME ONE STEP AT A TIME ONE STEP AT A TIME ONE STEP AT A TIME ONE STEP AT A TIME
ONE STEP AT A TIME ONE STEP AT A TIME ONE STEP AT A TIME ONE STEP AT A TIME ONE STEP AT A TIME
ONE STEP AT A TIME ONE STEP AT A TIME ONE STEP AT A TIME ONE STEP AT A TIME ONE STEP AT A TIME
ONE STEP AT A TIME ONE STEP AT A TIME ONE STEP AT A TIME ONE STEP AT A TIME ONE STEP AT A TIME
ONE STEP AT A TIME ONE STEP AT A TIME ONE STEP AT A TIME ONE STEP AT A TIME ONE STEP AT A TIME
ONE STEP AT A TIME ONE STEP AT A TIME ONE STEP AT A TIME ONE STEP AT A TIME ONE STEP AT A TIME
ONE STEP AT A TIME ONE STEP AT A TIME ONE STEP AT A TIME ONE STEP AT A TIME ONE STEP AT A TIME

ES, NOW! RIGHT NOW!" WHEN IT comes to issues of Spiritual growth, it's amazing how impatient (and childlike!) we are. Because of our impatience, we are so hard on ourselves, so hard on others, so hard on God. It is clear that learning the art of patience is a critical factor in ending the struggle and dancing with life.

Therefore, it is important that I leave you with some suggestions as to how to ease your sense of frustration when things are not going the way you want them to go, or when you think that you are not progressing far enough in healing your emotional wounds, or when you think that you've worked hard and nothing seems to be happening.

First, I want to remind you of the characteristics of Spiritual growth.

SPIRITUAL GROWTH IS SLOW. There are no quick fixes that I know of. There are quick and easy tools, but they are meant to be used for a lifetime. And there are sometimes amazing flashes of insight. But they usually are a result of years of unconscious or conscious seeking.

WHEN WE THINK NOTHING IS HAPPENING, IT IS. There is always an unseen world of energy moving and changing within and around us. *Trust* is the essential ingredient for feeling peaceful while these unseen forces do their work.

SPIRITUAL GROWTH IS NOT LINEAR. It has its spurts, its plateaus, and its backsteps. This is not to be lamented; it is just the way it is. And there is nothing to do about it but *let it be*.

SPIRITUAL GROWTH IS NEVER-ENDING. Never-ending means that there is always much more to learn; you never "get there."

> **Spiritual growth is not a destination. It is a forever process of learning and expanding and exploring and discovering. Therefore, when you focus on the goal, your attention is misplaced.**

If you put these four reminders always in your view, they may give you comfort during these disturbing times when impatience gets in the way of peace.

Nature is an incredible teacher of patience as it so beautifully demonstrates these characteristics of Spiritual growth. We watch the winter come and bring with it a barrenness of seemingly dead plants and trees. Just when it seems that spring will never come again, a miracle happens—a tiny bud appears on one of the barren trees. And little by little, step by step, as the sun warms and the rain nourishes, everything comes to life. The wondrous activity of summer surrounds us. Everything is alive.

We see dahlias and cosmos reaching four feet tall, roses spreading five inches in diameter, wisteria vines climbing up, down, and sideways, trees bearing fruit. And on and on and on. Looking at the barren winter, one could never envision such splendor arising from the earth.

Then the fall arrives. Magnificent golds and oranges and reds fill our vision as the sun's rays sparkle through the leaves. And we watch the leaves slowly dropping away to make way for another season of the life process. Soon the barrenness of winter comes upon us again. It's as though the trees and flowers have "returned to mountain," retreating, and waiting for their time to shine once again. From nature we learn to let go and allow things to happen in their own perfect time by simply watching how seeds hidden beneath the earth emerge to create bowers of beauty. We learn the concept of "This too shall pass" by watching storms turn into sunshine and sunshine turn into storms. We learn about ups and downs by watching the rhythms, the cycles, the ebb and flow, the harmony and the interplay of all things in nature. Even the most cynical among us has to be astounded by it all.

You can see that by really paying attention, *noticing* the cycles of nature, we learn all we need to know about the growth process and our impatience subsides, at least for the moment.

We always have to remember that we are part of nature. We seem to have forgotten this very important piece of reality. What makes remembering difficult is that we live in an instant world where everything has speeded up beyond our grasp. But *we are not instant people,* and that is where much of the confusion lies. Yes, there are many things that can be done speedily, but when it comes to Spiritual growth, the pace is slow. That's just the way it is.

From nature we also learn many principles of trust. As I stated earlier, trust is a very important factor in dealing with our impatience. In fact,

When we are impatient, it means we have no trust!

From nature, we learn that within and around us there are unseen forces that we can tap into to help us on our Journey. If we plant our seeds and tend our garden of life, the unseen forces will do their work, just as they do in nature.

As a patience exercise, plant a few seeds in a little flowerpot and watch the nothingness turn into something as grand as a beautiful flower. This simple process helps you develop trust in the life force. And every day as you water and care for your new symbol of this life force that lives within and around you, I suggest you say the following affirmation of trust to bring the message home:

As the life force is working to make my plant grow and radiate beauty into this world, so, too, the life force is working to make me grow and radiate beauty into this world. As I fill my plants with love, nourishment, and light, I commit to filling my life with love, nourishment, and light. I trust that as I do this, in exactly the right time, the light from my Higher Self will burst forth and show me the way.

This simple ritual will remind us to keep turning things over to our Higher Self or a Higher Power or both. In the beginning, we may turn it over but then take it back. We have to keep practicing turning it over and turning it over and turning it over, until we no longer take it back. When this happens, we know the true meaning of peace.

The part of us that keeps us from trusting is, of course, our Lower Self. The negative chatter in our mind, which comes from the Lower Self, takes all our peace away. At such times, it is necessary to say a few affirmations that replace this negativity with soothing thoughts of power and love. For example,

It's all happening perfectly for my highest good.
I can handle whatever happens in my life.
I have done my best and I let go of the outcome.

As you repeat these affirmations over and over again, you notice the sense of calm that comes over you. This sense of calm means that your Higher Self, your source of power and love, has come to the forefront. And it is in the Higher Self that the principle of trust finds its home.

So you see how nature can be one of our greatest teachers when it comes to matters of patience and trust. It wasn't so long ago that I didn't understand the big deal about nature. I had the attitude, "If you've seen one beautiful tree, you've seen them all." But when I finally stopped to look, I was overwhelmed by the splendor and mystery of it all. It reminds me to be overwhelmed by the splendor and mystery of my own place on this planet as well.

To further help you learn the art of patience, I suggest you study the teachings of the Tao. Of all the Eastern philosophies, the one that teaches us the most about patience is Taoism. It is from the Tao that tai chi and other reminders of our true nature can be found. Its principles are derived from the Tao Te Ching, which was written more than twenty-five hundred years ago by a man named Lao Tzu. As Diane Dreher tells us:

> "The Tao teaches patience, precision, and timing. Detaching from problems, we discover solutions. We learn to stop resisting and flow with the natural patterns, bringing greater joy and harmony to our lives."[2]

The Tao teaches us that all of life is process. It doesn't pay to be impatient since we can't change the rhythms, the patterns, the cycles, that are inherent in all of life. It can lead only to frustration.

Another way to bring patience into your life is to see yourself as a PERPETUAL BEGINNER. This is one time when being a beginner is better than being an expert! If we truly saw ourselves as perpetual beginners, we would automatically understand that we always have much more to learn. We would automatically understand that we won't always get it right. We would automatically understand that the way isn't always smooth. We would automatically know that we can't be expected to be perfect. As a result,

If we saw ourselves as perpetual beginners, we would be much kinder to ourselves.

We would see ourselves as little children learning and growing every step of the way. Naturally, we would be much kinder to others as well, understanding that they, too, are perpetual beginners and they won't always get it right.

W. Dean La Douceur really absorbed this message in one of my workshops and composed a wonderful poem he graciously allowed me to share with you. It has so much relevance here.

BABY STEPS

baby steps. personal small incremental steps. eyes open. feet propelling me forward. moving in a new direction.

baby steps. soft feet. new shoes. wobbly knees. progress.

baby steps. the need to move with care. move with grace. move with courage. move into a new direction. move against the wind. move unlike I've ever moved before. move and it's okay.

baby steps. soft light touch. soft light weight. soft light motions. soft light meanings. soft light fear. soft light power.

baby steps. the magical present-tense moment in my life when the hips move, the knees solidify from their weakness, and I am able to articulate my whole leg in a clearly desired direction of my choice without fear, chains, strings, or bondage, and move quickly each leg in motion with the other leg, foot, knee, and ankle in the same emotional, physical, biochemical, and spiritual process until I achieve momentum, force, power, speed, and light.

baby steps. looking back on the journey. recalling the fears which I moved past. reminding myself of the obstacles which I overcame. tapping into the victorious spirit. feeling the joyful rush.

baby steps. smiling. sharing. going. growing. flowing. loving. celebrating. pausing.

soon the time has come once again for me to take more baby steps.[3]

How wonderful! Dean's poem points out so vividly and gently that life is simply about the little baby steps that are always propelling us forward into new adventures. But it's *all* baby steps. We never "arrive." There is always something more to learn.

As I said earlier, despite all the advertisements for quick fixes, I know of none that really exists. If I find one, I'll certainly let you know. In the meantime, we need to learn to be happy with our baby steps. And if we learn to jump up and down for joy with each little step forward, *we are guaranteed to have a wonderful time along the way!*

There is something else you need to know. As you take your baby steps forward, you will notice that there are different *stages of understanding* on the Spiritual Journey. You will notice that in the beginning you KNOW on an intellectual level, but you don't yet FEEL on an emotional level. You know a certain truth, but you don't yet seem to be able to make it work in your life. For example, you *know* the concept of LET GO, but still you find yourself hanging on ever so tightly. Don't get discouraged. You are definitely on the right track.

I have heard students of great teachers express their disappointment when they discover that their teachers' lives are just as messed up as theirs. That is, that they aren't "walking their talk." Don't be disappointed if you make such a discovery! Some of the greatest teachers I have ever had were still operating their lives from the level of the mind. That is, they knew on an intellectual level what is truth on a Spiritual level; they just hadn't internalized these great truths. Their Lower Self, which houses the qualities of ego, greed, and fear, was still getting in the way. *That doesn't necessarily make their teachings any less valid.*

When I started teaching I didn't yet *feel*, but I *knew*. As the saying goes, "We teach best what we want to learn most." A wonderful story that I heard from Marilyn Ferguson, author of *the Aquarian Conspiracy*,[4] comes to mind. A professor describes his teaching a new concept to his class. "I told them once; they didn't understand. I told them twice; they didn't understand. I told them three times . . . and *I* understood." This certainly was my experience. Through my own repetition of the concepts and tools, I eventually *lived into* the emotional understanding of many of them, although I still have a long way to go on many of the others. This is why my husband teases me when I am lamenting a problem, "Go read your book!" And he is right. More repetition is necessary on my part.

After a certain period of knowing but not yet feeling, you notice that you have flashes of clarity in your everyday life. This clarity is not something that can be sustained on a regular basis in the beginning. Back to our earlier example, you notice you are able to LET GO in certain areas of your life some of the time. This is great progress. Again, with attention and repetition of the various Spiritual tools available to you, the balance on the scales starts to shift. More and more you have clarity and less and less you have confusion.

At some point you begin to think you are truly living with great understanding, but you may not be seeing yourself clearly. One clue that you haven't quite internalized the lessons is that you become righteous and judgmental of others who don't believe as you do. The more clarity you get, the less righteous and judgmental you become.

Another thing that happens in the process of our Spiritual growth is that as the voice of the Higher Self gets louder, so does the voice of the Lower Self. For example, as feelings of power come up, a minute later the feelings of wanting to be taken care of also come up. The Lower Self doesn't want to give up any control and so it has to be humored sometimes. But after a while, the Lower Self sees the writing on the wall and retreats, leaving the Higher Self to be heard loud and clear, at least for a while.

At first you will think of the Spiritual Journey as only a small part of your life: for example, twenty minutes of meditation or tai chi in the morning. Eventually, the lessons start inserting themselves profoundly in the way we relate to people and the world around us. And we know that in that particular area of our growth, we are making significant headway.

Many of us experience great procrastination in starting or continuing the Spiritual Journey. This is because we have to give up familiar ways of being in the world in order to move forward. This feels scary! Even if these ways of being are giving us nothing but aggravation, at least we know what we are going to get! Aggravation seems less frightening than the unknown. So we make excuses that stop us from moving full steam ahead. For example,

WE PRETEND THAT OUR LIVES ARE TOO BUSY. What can be more important than learning how to live our lives fully and joyfully? Add to this the fact that many of our Spiritual tools can be incorporated very easily into our everyday lives. For example, affirmations take no time at all. All we have to do is insert positive thoughts when the negative ones are making us miserable!

WE CAN'T BEGIN BECAUSE OUR LIFE IS SUCH A MESS. Can you think of a better time to begin? The most moving example of people starting their Spiritual Journey when their lives were a mess comes from the prison ashram project which you can read about in Bo Lozoff's book, *We're All Doing Time*.[5] Here, prisoners, some incarcerated for the remainder of their lives or on death row, discovered a Spiritual path through meditation that transformed their life of Hell to one that is closer to Heaven.

IT'S TOO CONFUSING; WE DON'T KNOW WHERE TO BEGIN. I am going to take that excuse away from you and show you where to begin.

It is true that today's world offers a huge variety of tools to help us on our Spiritual Journey. While we would all like to find a surrogate parent out there to take our hand and tell us which one to pick, that person doesn't exist. No one out there knows what is right for us. Only we can determine this for ourselves.

And the way we determine the path that is right for us is to take those wonderful baby steps. We experiment. We try different things. Sometimes we'll like what we get; sometimes we won't. But it's all part of the banquet called LIFE. Sometimes we have to acquire a taste for certain things that don't "taste" right in the beginning.

Once we get past the initial discomfort, we often like the taste. Sometimes we don't, and it is wise to travel on.

Your entry into a Spiritual path could be as simple as going to a bookstore and looking in the self-help, New Age, and psychology sections. Pick a book that "speaks to you" or draws your attention. Or your entry could be volunteering to serve others, such as helping to prepare lunches for those who have no food. Or it could be meditation if you feel the need for quieting the mind. Or it could be affirmation tapes to help you begin to eradicate the negativity of the chatter in your mind. Or all of the above.

Each is an entry point into another way of seeing. Follow *your* heart, no one else's. You will notice that one avenue leads to another, which leads to another, which leads to another. Just keep remembering that the teachings are all around you. You have only to take that first step. And it could be a very small step indeed. Don't pressure yourself. Just listen to yourself. Ask your Higher Self to show you the way. And just follow those inner directions.

I suggest starting with those Spiritual tools that are easy for you. Quieting my mind was very difficult for me in the beginning, so I didn't start my Spiritual Journey with meditation. I was drawn more to affirmations, guided visualizations, books, and workshops. Later I found myself drawn to meditation. I was "ready." So, in the beginning, be a student of what attracts you.

Some may dictate that you should do it this way or that way. For you, there is only one way, *your way*. This isn't to say that you can't use the advice of teachers. They can point us in many directions that we wouldn't have taken without their guidance. But it is up to us to sift and pick what works for us and what doesn't, and for how long. When I approach a new teacher, it is with the thought that I will take what works for me and let the rest go. I ask you to approach your teachers, including myself, in the same way. Take what seems right for you and leave the rest behind.

When others try to impose their will, don't get defensive. Simply say, "Thanks for sharing your ideas," and then go on to do what feels right for you. Sometimes this takes a lot of courage, but *FEEL THE FEAR AND DO WHAT FEELS RIGHT FOR YOU ANY- WAY!* If you encounter any person (or organization) who says, "This is the *only* way," turn on your heels and run the other way. There are many ways to your heart, to love, to trust, to peace, to God.

On your Spiritual Journey, a teacher can be considered anyone or anything that helps you. It could be your child, a sunset, a tape, a book, a flower, an illness, or whatever we are presented with in the course of our everyday lives. Teachers point us in the right direction. It's up to us to take the necessary steps forward.

You may notice that many turn their lives over to "gurus" who are supposed to be fully enlightened beings. By definition, this doesn't work. First, it is questionable whether any truly enlightened beings exist. (Again, if I find any, I'll let you know.) Second, any time we turn our lives over to any other person, we are giving our power away, power to create a life that truly works for who we are as human beings.

Since I've never met a truly enlightened being, I see a guru not as a reality but as a model of what direction I need to be going. For example, I see the sculpture of the laughing Buddha that sits on my desk as a model of the state of pure joy and awareness and simplicity. I may never attain it, but just looking at his face every morning points me in the right direction. I've trained myself not to have the expectation that I will eventually arrive at the state of spiritual grace that his face radiates. If I do, that is wonderful. If I don't, that is wonderful as well. I'm enjoying the baby steps along the way.

Once you find a certain method of Spiritual growth, such as meditation or tai chi, that appeals to you, do you stay with it or do you try others as well? Again, it's up to you. I'm a flitter. I love to try different methods no matter how strange some of them may seem. I've gone to India with a Jain monk and some of his followers. I've gone to the pyramids in Egypt with a group of meditators. I've stud- ied visualizations, body work, scream therapy, chanting, Eastern philosophies, many types of group participation, and on and on. I've *loved* the whole process of exploration. *Ultimately, it all seems to fit into one encompassing whole.* One day in the future I may find a method that I choose to stick with and let all the rest go. That remains to be seen.

There are those who decry flitting from one method to another. They feel it's best to stay with a method, and for them this is the approach that works. The point is to feel what is right for you and go with it. If you find a method of Spiritual growth that works for you and you want to continue with it, then continue with it. If you feel you have tried a method, gotten a lot out of it, but it is now time to move on to another, then move on to another. You may find yourself returning to it at a later time, or you may not. If you feel a method is totally wrong for you right from the beginning, move on to another method.

Trust you know what is right for you at any particular time.

If you don't trust what is right for you, ask your Higher Self to show you the way. THEN PAY ATTENTION! So many times we don't listen to our intuition even though it is sending us valuable messages. One guaranteed way to know that you are on an appropriate path is to ask yourself, "Does this path have a heart? Does what I am trying to do bring more love and caring into the world?"

And don't worry about taking the "wrong" road. That happens sometimes. If we learn and grow, even from our mistakes, then they aren't mistakes. We are learning every step of the way. All parts of our lives can be used to help the Spiritual part of who we are come forward and enrich our lives. This is a relief. We don't have to know all the answers. We don't have to work for an A as we did in school. We don't have to be afraid to make mistakes. In fact, in *Feel the Fear and Do It Anyway*, I remind people,

"If you haven't made any mistakes lately, you must be doing something wrong!"

Mistakes suggest that we are learning and growing and experimenting and expanding in life, and we won't always get it right.

Also remember that upset in your life is not a sign that something has gone wrong, only that something is changing. Change usually brings confusion. But one day we live into clarity once again, at least for a while, until the next change in our life, which brings us back into a state of confusion. Confusion and clarity, confusion and clarity, confusion and clarity seems to be the rhythm of growth. In that, confusion is not a bad thing!

Let me debunk a popular myth about Spiritual growth, which is, "When we are spiritually evolved, no manner of harm shall come into our lives." This myth creates a feeling of guilt if "bad" things happen to us, as if we did something wrong. I don't believe this myth at all. I believe that . . .

"Bad" things happen to all of us, whether we are spiritually evolving or not.

Into each life falls loss, illness, confusion, conflict, and so on. That is the nature of life on this planet. The difference is that . . .

When we are spiritually evolving, we are in a better place to handle whatever life hands us.

And that's what ending the struggle and dancing with life is all about—handling all that happens to us in a loving and powerful way, knowing we will find some wonderful piece of wisdom from it all. If we have the patience to sit there with the attitude of, "Aha! I wonder what this experience is going to teach me," then we can live more with a spirit of mystery and adventure rather than with a feeling of fear and helplessness and impatience.

Ultimately, we learn that there are no shortcuts. The process is the process and there's not much we can do about it. We all want the quick and easy, but when it comes to becoming a Spiritual being, speed doesn't work. We are going for a deep change in the depths of our being. This is a lifetime process.

Martial arts expert Joe Hyams tells us the formula one of his teachers gave to him:

"To give yourself time is to actively work toward a goal without setting a limit on how long you will work."[6]

I like that. In a world of deadlines and stress, it is wonderful to know that there is one area in our life where *it is better not to rush,* and that is the area of Spiritual growth. Hyams recounts a wonderful old tale that describes the difference between the present-day thinking of "Try harder!" and the ancient wisdom of how to obtain true mastery. Really take in the meaning of this story.

A young boy traveled across Japan to study with a famous martial artist. The master asked him what he wanted. The young boy told him he wanted to be the finest martial artist in the land and asked how long he had to study. "Ten years at least," the master answered. "But what if I studied twice as hard as all your other students," the young boy responded. "Twenty years," replied the master. "Twenty years! What if I practice day and night with all my effort?" "Thirty years," was the master's reply. The boy was thoroughly confused. "How is it that each time I say I will work harder, you tell me that it will take longer?" the boy asked. "The answer is clear. When one eye is fixed upon your destination, there is only one eye left with which to find the Way."[7]

A great story. How *can* we look mindfully and deeply when one eye is on the goal? How *can* we learn the art of letting go when one eye is on the goal? How *can* we learn the art of embracing all that is beautiful in life when one eye is on the goal? The answer is simple— we can't. So decide that you are going to do it with both eyes on the process and forget about the goal! I know this contradicts so much of your previous teaching, but in the area of Spiritual growth, you have entered a new dimension of being.

When you stop thinking that you have to do it all now, or even in this lifetime, your impatience dissolves into the sweet flow that is the natural rhythm of life. And as you continue your step-by-step journey, inward and upward to the best of who we are, life just gets better and better and better and better.

Questions will always come up. Don't drive yourself crazy trying to find the answers. Many questions have no answers. When the mistrust of the Lower Self wants to know why, simply tell it, "Because." No need to explain any further than that. From the perspective of the Higher Self, it's all about *trust*. Perhaps one day you will live into the answers, perhaps you won't. In truth, it really doesn't matter. When trust is there, your life works beautifully whether you know the answers or not.

I have lived into many answers over the course of my lifetime, and I still live with many questions. But finding answers isn't so important to me any more. As I increase my trust in the Grand Design, I know that it's all happening perfectly, in its own time and in its own way. And I have learned to live very peacefully with that.

COMMIT COMMIT COMMIT COMMIT COMMIT COMMIT COMMIT COMMIT COMMIT COMMIT COMMIT
COMMIT COMMIT COMMIT COMMIT COMMIT COMMIT COMMIT COMMIT COMMIT COMMIT COMMIT
COMMIT COMMIT COMMIT COMMIT COMMIT COMMIT COMMIT COMMIT COMMIT COMMIT COMMIT
COMMIT COMMIT COMMIT COMMIT COMMIT COMMIT COMMIT COMMIT COMMIT COMMIT COMMIT
COMMIT COMMIT COMMIT COMMIT COMMIT COMMIT COMMIT COMMIT COMMIT COMMIT COMMIT
COMMIT COMMIT COMMIT COMMIT COMMIT COMMIT COMMIT COMMIT COMMIT COMMIT COMMIT

A CLOSING MESSAGE

NOTHING CAN STOP YOU NOW!

COMMIT COMMIT COMMIT COMMIT COMMIT COMMIT COMMIT COMMIT COMMIT COMMIT COMMIT
COMMIT COMMIT COMMIT COMMIT COMMIT COMMIT COMMIT COMMIT COMMIT COMMIT COMMIT
COMMIT COMMIT COMMIT COMMIT COMMIT COMMIT COMMIT COMMIT COMMIT COMMIT COMMIT
COMMIT COMMIT COMMIT COMMIT COMMIT COMMIT COMMIT COMMIT COMMIT COMMIT COMMIT
COMMIT COMMIT COMMIT COMMIT COMMIT COMMIT COMMIT COMMIT COMMIT COMMIT COMMIT
COMMIT COMMIT COMMIT COMMIT COMMIT COMMIT COMMIT COMMIT COMMIT COMMIT COMMIT
COMMIT COMMIT COMMIT COMMIT COMMIT COMMIT COMMIT COMMIT COMMIT COMMIT COMMIT
COMMIT COMMIT COMMIT COMMIT COMMIT COMMIT COMMIT COMMIT COMMIT COMMIT COMMIT
COMMIT COMMIT COMMIT COMMIT COMMIT COMMIT COMMIT COMMIT COMMIT COMMIT COMMIT
COMMIT COMMIT COMMIT COMMIT COMMIT COMMIT COMMIT COMMIT COMMIT COMMIT COMMIT
COMMIT COMMIT COMMIT COMMIT COMMIT COMMIT COMMIT COMMIT COMMIT COMMIT COMMIT
COMMIT COMMIT COMMIT COMMIT COMMIT COMMIT COMMIT COMMIT COMMIT COMMIT COMMIT
COMMIT COMMIT COMMIT COMMIT COMMIT COMMIT COMMIT COMMIT COMMIT COMMIT COMMIT
COMMIT COMMIT COMMIT COMMIT COMMIT COMMIT COMMIT COMMIT COMMIT COMMIT COMMIT
COMMIT COMMIT COMMIT COMMIT COMMIT COMMIT COMMIT COMMIT COMMIT COMMIT COMMIT
COMMIT COMMIT COMMIT COMMIT COMMIT COMMIT COMMIT COMMIT COMMIT COMMIT COMMIT
COMMIT COMMIT COMMIT COMMIT COMMIT COMMIT COMMIT COMMIT COMMIT COMMIT COMMIT
COMMIT COMMIT COMMIT COMMIT COMMIT COMMIT COMMIT COMMIT COMMIT COMMIT COMMIT
COMMIT COMMIT COMMIT COMMIT COMMIT COMMIT COMMIT COMMIT COMMIT COMMIT COMMIT

I HAVE PRESENTED MANY IDEAS throughout the chapters of this book—all meant to show you that you have the power to create more and more exquisite moments in your life. These exquisite moments come with the creation of an inner trust—trust in the process, trust in yourself, and trust in the Divine Mystery of it all.

You deserve the best that life has to offer. And it's reassuring to know that you don't have to go outside yourself to find the best; it lies within your very being. The best is your Higher Self, the part of you that sees everything as a glorious adventure, the part of you that embraces the abundance of gifts that are placed before you, the part of you that notices and is grateful for the miracle of it all, the part of you that knows that you are a vibrantly meaningful part of the Grand Design.

The most important thing you can do for yourself is to follow the Path that takes you to the best of who you are. Finding the enormous amount of power and love that lies within is the secret to ending the struggle and dancing with life.

So COMMIT to this wonderful Journey of discovery! Remember . . .

Commitment creates a powerful radiant energy that acti-vates all sorts of "miracles" within and around you.

I've seen these miracles in my life, and you will see them in yours. Trust me when I tell you that there is NOTHING that can stop you once you make that commitment to create a life of trust, peace, beauty, lightness, abundance, love, and joy!

Embrace the Journey . . .
Embrace who you are . . .
Embrace all there is . . .

From my heart to yours,

Susan Jeffers

CHAPTER NOTES

Introduction
1. Bo Lozoff, *We're All Doing Time* (Durham, NC: Human Kindness Foundation, 1985).

Chapter 1
1. Nikos Kazantzakis, *Zorba the Greek* (New York: Simon & Schuster, 1953), p. 8.
2. Ram Dass, *Finding and Exploring Your Spiritual Path* (Audio Renaissance Tapes, 1989).

Chapter 2
1. Ken Keyes Jr., *How to Enjoy Your Life in Spite of It All* (St. Mary, KY: Living Love Publications, 1980), p. 5.

Chapter 3
1. Bill Naughton, *Alfie*, Paramount Pictures, 1966.
2. *Webster's College Dictionary* (New York: Random House, 1991).
3. Walter Cooper, *Shards: Restoring the Shattered Spirit* (Deerfield Beach, FL: Health Communications, 1992), p. 125.
4. Ram Dass, *Who Are You?* (Arlington, VA: The Soundworks). In *Dare to Connect* I discuss in detail how our "Somebody Training" badly undermines our confidence as we reach out to others in romance, friendship, and the workplace. I suggest a much more powerful alternative.
5. Alfie Kohn demonstrates in his fascinating book *No Contest: The Case Against Competition* (Boston: Houghton Mifflin, 1986), that in every study ever done on the subject, competition diminishes performance; it doesn't enhance it. Partnership and cooperation produce the best results.
6. I am deeply grateful to James W. Steen for giving me permission to share his wonderful insights with you.
7. Lozoff, *We're All Doing Time*, p. 4.

Chapter 4
1. To find out about Workaholics Anonymous, call or write their central office at P.O. Box 289, Menlo Park, CA 94026-0289 (510) 273-9253. In addition to giving you information, they will help you determine if there is a Workaholics Anonymous group in your area.
2. Gore Vidal, quoted in *Newsweek*, March 25, 1968.
3. Jann Mitchell, *Organized Serenity: How to Manage Your Time and Life in Recovery* (Deerfield Beach, FL: Health Communications, 1992), p. 33.

4. Linda Weltner, "The Joys of Mediocrity," *New Age Journal*, September/October 1993, p. 168.

Chapter 5

1. To find out about Co-Dependents Anonymous (CoDa), write or call Co-Dependents Anonymous, Inc., P.O. Box 33577, Phoenix, AZ 85067-3577 (602) 277-7991. In addition to giving you information, they will help you determine if there is a CoDa group in your area.
2. Susan Jeffers, *Dare to Connect: Reaching Out in Romance, Friendship, and the Workplace* (New York: Fawcett, 1992), Chapter 8.
3. Barry Stevens, *Burst Out Laughing* (Berkeley: Celestial Arts, 1984), p. 20.
4. Joe Dominguez and Vicki Robbin, *Your Money or Your Life: Transforming Your Relationship with Money and Achieving Financial Independence* (New York: Viking, Penguin 1993).
5. From an interview in *Mirabella*, May 1993, p. 158.

Chapter 6

1. Stevens, *Burst Out Laughing*, p. 35.
2. *The Journey from Lost to Found: The Search That Begins with the End of a Relationship* (New York: Fawcett, 1993) chronicles my personal search for wholeness when my first marriage ended many years ago. It might offer healing reassurance if you or a loved one is experiencing the painful end of a relationship.
3. These questions are asked of God in *A Course in Miracles*, Volume 2, *A Workbook for Students* (Foundation for Inner Peace, P.O. Box 635, Tiburon, CA 94920, p. 121). In Chapter 14, I describe my sense of the connection between our Higher Self and a Higher Power.
4. Barry Stevens, *Don't Push the River: It Flows by Itself* (Moab, UT: Real People Press, 1970).

Chapter 7

1. Alan Cohen, *Joy Is My Compass* (Port Huron: MI: Alan Cohen Publications, 1990), pp. 9-12. For a free catalog of Alan Cohen's books, tapes, and workshop schedules, write to RLS, P.O. Box 5030, Port Huron, MI 48061-5031, or call (800) 462-3013. I thank Alan for his input and his permission to use his wonderful story.
2. Charles J. Sykes, *A Nation of Victims: The Decay of the American Character* (New York: St. Martin's Press, 1992), p. 12.
3. In *Opening Our Hearts to Men: Learn to Let Go of Anger, Pain, and Loneliness and Create a Love That Works* (New York: Fawcett, 1989), which is about taking charge of our lives and honoring who we are, I elaborate on how the principle of "picking up the mirror instead of the magnifying glass" can strengthen us in all areas of our lives.
4. I invite you to read Chapter 8 in my book *Dare to Connect* to evaluate what constitutes a healthy group process.

5. Wayne Muller, *Legacy of the Heart: The Spiritual Advantages of a Painful Childhood* (New York: Simon & Schuster, 1992).

Chapter 8

1. Chungliang Al Huang, *Quantum Soup: Fortune Cookies in Crisis* (Berkeley: Celestial Arts, 1991), p. 59.
2. Used with permission from Kenneth Cole.
3. Michael Ventura, "The Earthquake People," *Psychology Today*, May/June 1994, p. 14.
4. Joan Borysenko, *Fire in the Soul: A New Psychology of Spiritual Optimism* (New York: Warner Books, 1993).

Chapter 9

1. Jeffers, *The Journey from Lost to Found*, p. 152.
2. Many tools for healing the pain that lies inside are found in this book as well as my previous books, *Feel the Fear and Do It Anyway*, *Opening Our Hearts to Men*, and *Dare to Connect*.
3. This is adapted from a quote of George Bernard Shaw in *Man and Superman* (London: Penguin Books, 1903), p. 32.
4. Sam Keen describes "psychological numbing" in *The Passionate Life: Stages of Loving* (New York: Harper, 1983).
5. Huang, *Quantum Soup*, p. 14.
6. Stephen Levine, *Meetings at the Edge: Dialogues with the Grieving and the Dying, the Healing and the Healed* (New York: Doubleday, 1984).
7. "Somewhere Out There" is from *An American Tail* (music from the motion picture soundtrack), MCA, performed by Linda Ronstadt and James Ingram, 1986.

Chapter 11

1. Benjamin Hoff, *The Tao of Pooh* (New York: Penguin Books, 1982), p. xi.
2. Zalman Schachter-Shalomi, *The Spiritual Elder: How to Enjoy the Harvest of a Lifetime* (Boulder, CO: Sounds True Recordings).
3. For a catalog of Esalen workshops, write to Esalen Institute, Big Sur, CA 93920.
4. Chogyam Trungpa, *Shambhala: The Sacred Path of the Warrior* (New York: Bantam Books, 1984), p. 29.

Chapter 12

1. Brother David Steindl-Rast, *The Grateful Heart* (Boulder CO: Sounds True Recordings, 1992).
2. Rob Eichberg is the author of *Coming Out: An Act of Love* (New York: Dutton Books, 1990).
3. Deepak Chopra, *The Return of the Rishi* (Boston: Houghton Mifflin, 1988), p. 117.

4. David K. Reynolds, *A Thousand Waves: A Sensible Life Style for Sensitive People* (New York: William Morrow, 1990), p. 31.
5. You can get information about The Inside Edge by calling (310) 281-8933 (Los Angeles).
6. The audiotape and book *Inner Talk for a Confident Day* can be obtained from Hay House, P.O. Box 6204, Dept. SJ, Carson, CA 90749-6204 (1-800) 654-5126. Or it can be ordered from most bookstores.
7. Noah benShea, *Jacob's Journey* (New York: Ballantine Books, 1991), pp. 47, 49.
8. Viktor Frankl, *Man's Search for Meaning* (New York: Simon & Schuster, 1939), p. 61.

Chapter 13

1. For more information about TM, read *Happiness: The TM Program, Psychiatry and Enlightenment* by Harold H. Bloomfield, M.D., and Robert B. Kory (New York: Simon & Schuster, 1976) and *Transcendental Meditation* by Robert Roth (New York: Donald I. Fine, 1987).
2. Denise Denniston and Peter McWilliams, *The TM Book: How to Enjoy the Rest of Your Life* (Allen Park, MI: Three Rivers Press, 1975), p. 52.
3. Roth, *Transcendental Meditation*, p. 18.
4. Leon Weiner is a teacher associated with the Santa Fe Transcendental Meditation Center, 111 Spruce Street, Santa Fe, NM 87501.
5. Louise Hay, *The Power Is Within You* (Carson, CA: Hay House, 1991), p. 43.
6. For an explanation and sample of guided visualizations, listen to the unabridged audiotapes of *Feel the Fear and Do It Anyway* and *Dare to Connect*. The guided visualizations are heard on the second side of the last tape. Audiotapes can be obtained from Hay House, P.O. Box 6204, Carson, CA 90749-6204 (1-800) 654-5126. There are also many audiotapes on the market that feature guided visualizations. They are very effective for those who have difficulty quieting the mind.
7. Gerald Jampolsky and Diane Cirincione share this quip of the noted authors Hugh and Gayle Prather in their videotape *Another Way of Looking at the World*, available from Hay House, P.O. Box 6204, Carson CA 90749-6204 (1-800) 654-5126.
8. Stuart Wilde, *Miracles* (Taos, NM: White Dover International, 1983), p. 7.
9. J. Krishnamurti, *Freedom from the Known* (New York: Harper, 1969), p. 10.
10. Franz Kafka, *The Great Wall of China* (Prague: Heinr. Mercy Sohn, 1936, 1937. Copyright 1946 by Schocken Books, Random House, New York), p. 184.

Chapter 14

1. Larry Dossey, M.D., provides compelling evidence about the power of prayer in *Healing Words: The Power of Prayer and the Practice of Medicine* (San Francisco: Harper, 1993).
2. I suggest that you read *Illuminata: Thoughts, Prayers, Rites of Passage* by Marianne Williamson (New York: Random House, 1994). It is a beautiful book

that offers further insights into the use of prayer. Many examples of meaningful prayers are given.

Chapter 15

1. Thomas F. Crum, *The Magic of Conflict* (New York: Simon & Schuster, 1987), p. 15.
2. Chungliang Al Huang, *Tai Ji: Beginner's Tai Ji Book* (Berkeley: Celestial Arts, 1989), p. 31.
3. Ibid., p. 24.
4. The concept of Divine Homesickness is derived from the work of Roberto Assagioli, founder of the psychological school of psychosynthesis.
5. Jeffers, *Dare to Connect*, pp. 189-90.

Chapter 16

1. This quote of Rabindranath Tagore appears in *Noetic Sciences Review*, Spring 1994, Institute of Noetic Sciences, 475 Gate Five Road, Suite 300, Sausalito, CA 94965.
2. For information about Nikki Winston, her workshop schedule, or to purchase her excellent videotape *Tai Chi: The Golden Door's Response to Stress*, contact her through WIN International, 110 Fifteenth Street, Del Mar, CA 92014, or fax (619) 755-1811.
3. I also suggest you contact the Living Tao Foundation, from which you can get a catalog of the videotapes of Chungliang Al Huang, a renowned tai chi expert. You can also get a schedule of his workshops: P.O. Box 846, Urbana, IL 61801 (217) 337-6113. Huang has written some excellent books that are listed in the bibliography.
4. My thanks to Nikki Winston for an in-depth interview that contributed greatly to my knowledge about these metaphors of nature and tai chi.
5. Eva Wong, translator, *Seven Taoist Masters: A Folk Novel of China* (Boston: Shambhala Press, 1990), p. 52.

Chapter 17

1. Astarius Reiki-Om, *The New Mexican Newspaper*, Pasatiempo Section, July 16-22, 1993, p. 18. Astarius is a poet, astrologer, writer, and public speaker.
2. Howard Papush, for example, known nationally as "Dr. Play," teaches corporations and organizations throughout the country how to work together more effectively in a spirit of fun, lightness, and laughter. He can be contacted at Let's Play Again, 360 S. Burnside Avenue, Los Angeles, CA 90036 (213) 934-3888.
3. Robert A. Johnson, *Ecstasy: Understanding the Psychology of Joy* (San Francisco: Harper, 1987), p. 11.
4. Ibid., p. vii.
5. Thich Nhat Hanh, *Peace Is Every Step: The Path of Mindfulness in Everyday Life* (New York: Bantam Books, 1991).

6. Stevens, *Burst Out Laughing*, p. 97.
7. Huang, *Quantum Soup*, pp. 13, 14.
8. Chungliang Al Huang, *Embrace Tiger, Return to Mountain: Mythbody to Live By* (Berkeley: New Medicine Tapes). (1-800) 647-1110.
9. From an interview with Annette Goodheart, "Laugh Till You Cry," in *Association of Humanistic Psychology Newsletter*, July 1992, p. 12.
10. Ibid., p. 13.
11. Barry Neil Kaufman, *Happiness Is a Choice* (New York: Fawcett, 1991), p. 3. Kaufman and his wife teach their concepts about turning misery into happiness at the Option Institute, P.O. Box 1180, Sheffield, MA 01257 (413) 229-2100.
12. Jeffers, *Opening Our Hearts to Men*, Chapter 9.

Chapter 18
1. Jann Mitchell, *Codependent for Sure: An Original Jokebook* (Kansas City, MO: Andrews and McMeel, 1992), p. 94.
2. Diane Dreher, *The Tao of Inner Peace* (New York: Harper, 1990), p. xiii.
3. Reprinted by permission of W. Dean La Douceur, who is a consultant and the president of LBDS in Troy, Michigan, which provides services in marketing and communications.
4. Marilyn Ferguson, *The Aquarian Conspiracy* (Los Angeles: Jeremy P. Tarcher, 1980).
5. Lozoff, *We're All Doing Time*.
6. Joe Hyams, *Zen in the Martial Arts* (New York: Bantam Books, 1979), p. 16.
7. Ibid., p. 87.

SUGGESTED BOOKS AND AUDIOTAPES*

benShea, Noah. *Jacob's Journey*. New York: Ballantine Books, 1991.

Bloomfield, Harold H., and Robert K. Cooper. *The Power of Five*. Emmaus, PA: Rodale Press, 1995.

Bloomfield, Harold H., and Robert B. Kory. *Happiness: The TM Program, Psychiatry and Enlightenment*. New York: Simon & Schuster, 1976.

Borysenko, Joan. *Fire in the Soul: A New Psychology of Spiritual Optimism*. New York: Warner Books, 1993.

Canfield, Jack, and Mark Victor Hansen. *Chicken Soup for the Soul*. Deerfield Beach, FL: Health Communications, 1993.

Chopra, Deepak. *The Return of Merlin*. New York: Harmony Books, 1995.

————. *The Return of the Rishi*. Boston: Houghton Mifflin, 1988.

————. *The Seven Spiritual Laws of Success*. San Rafael, CA: Amber-Allen/New World Library, 1994.

Cohen, Alan. *Joy Is My Compass*. Alan Cohen Publications, RLS, P.O. Box 5030, Port Huron, MI 48061-5031 (800)462-3013, 1990.

Cooper, Walter. *Shards: Restoring the Shattered Spirit*. Deerfield Beach, FL: Health Communications, 1992.

A Course in Miracles. Foundation for Inner Peace, P.O. Box 635, Tiburon, CA 94920.

Cowan, John. *The Common Table: Reflections and Meditations on Community and Spirituality in the Workplace*. New York: Harper, 1993.

Crum, Thomas F. *The Magic of Conflict*. New York: Simon & Schuster, 1987.

Dass, Ram. *Finding and Exploring Your Spiritual Path*. Audio Renaissance Tapes, Inc., 1989. Audiotape.

————. *Who Are You?* The Soundworks, 911 N. Fillmore Street, Arlington, VA 22201. Audiotape.

De Angeles, Barbara. *Real Moments*. New York: Delacorte, 1994.

---

*This is a list of books and tapes included in the chapter notes plus other recommended books and tapes. They can be bought or ordered at your bookstore. Please note that books and tapes often go out of stock and are unavailable. Not to worry! There is always another to fill your needs.

Denniston, Denise, and Peter McWilliams. *The TM Book: How to Enjoy the Rest of Your Life.* Three Rivers Press, 5806 Elizabeth Street, Allen Park, MI 48101, 1975.

Dobson, Terry, and Victor Miller. *Aikido In Everyday Life: Giving in to Get Your Way.* Berkeley: North Atlantic Books, 1978.

Dominguez, Joe, and Vicki Robbin. *Your Money or Your Life: Transforming Your Relationship with Money and Achieving Financial Independence.* New York: Viking Penguin, 1993.

Dossey, Larry. *Healing Words: The Power of Prayer and the Practice of Medicine.* San Francisco: Harper 1993.

Dreher, Diane. *The Tao of Inner Peace.* New York: Harper, 1990.

Dyer, Wayne. *Real Magic: Creating Miracles in Everyday Life.* New York: Harper, 1992.

———. *Your Sacred Self.* New York: Harper, 1995.

Eichberg, Rob. *Coming Out: An Act of Love.* New York: Dutton Books, 1990.

Fassel, Diane. *Working Ourselves to Death: And the Rewards of Recovery.* New York: Harper, 1990.

Ferguson, Marilyn. *The Aquarian Conspiracy.* Los Angeles: Jeremy P. Tarcher, 1980.

Fields, Rick, with Peggy Taylor, Rex Weyler, and Rick Ingrasci. *Chop Wood, Carry Water: A Guide to Finding Spiritual Fulfillment in Everyday Life.* Los Angeles: Jeremy P. Tarcher, 1984.

Frankl, Viktor. *Man's Search for Meaning.* New York: Simon & Schuster, 1939.

Goldberg, Natalie. *Long Quiet Highway.* New York: Bantam Books, 1993.

Gordon, Sol, and Harold Brecher. *Life Is Uncertain . . . Eat Dessert First!: Finding the Joy You Deserve.* New York: Delacorte, 1990.

Hallstein, Richard W. *Memoirs of a Recovering Autocrat: Revealing Insights for Managing the Autocrat in All of Us.* San Francisco: Berrett-Koehler, 1992.

Hanh, Thich Nhat. *Peace Is Every Step: The Path of Mindfulness in Everyday Life.* New York: Bantam Books, 1991.

Hay, Louise. *The Power Is Within You.* Carson, CA: Hay House, 1991.

Hoff, Benjamin. *The Tao of Pooh.* New York: Penguin Books, 1982.

H.T.P. *Turning It Over: How to Find Tranquility When You Never Thought You Could.* Deerfield Beach, FL: Health Communications, 1992.

Huang, Chungliang Al. *Embrace Tiger, Return to Mountain: The Essence of Tai Ji.* Berkeley: Celestial Arts, 1973.

———. *Quantum Soup: Fortune Cookies in Crisis.* Berkeley: Celestial Arts, 1991.

———. *Tai Ji: Beginners Tai Ji Book.* Berkeley: Celestial Arts, 1989.

Hyams, Joe. *Zen in the Martial Arts.* New York: Bantam Books, 1979.

Jeffers, Susan. *Dare to Connect: Reaching Out in Romance, Friendship, and the Workplace.* New York: Fawcett, 1992. Unabridged audiotape. Carson, CA: Hay House.

———. *Feel the Fear and Do It Anyway: Dynamic Techniques for Turning Fear, Indecision, and Anger into Power, Action, and Love.* New York: Fawcett, 1987. Unabridged and abridged audiotape also available. Carson, CA: Hay House.

———. *Inner Talk for a Confident Day.* Carson, CA: Hay House. Book and audiotape available.

———. *The Journey from Lost to Found: The Search That Begins with the End of a Relationship.* New York: Fawcett, 1993.

———. *Opening Our Hearts to Men: Learn to Let Go of Anger, Pain, and Loneliness and Create a Love That Works.* New York: Fawcett, 1989. Unabridged audiotape also available. Carson, CA: Hay House.

———. *Thoughts of Power and Love.* Carson, CA: Hay House, 1995.

Johnson, Robert A. *Ecstasy: Understanding the Psychology of Joy.* San Francisco: Harper, 1987.

Kabat-Zinn, Jon. *Mindfulness Meditation for Everyday Life.* New York: Hyperion, 1994.

Kaufman, Barry Neil. *Happiness Is a Choice.* New York: Fawcett, 1991.

Kazantzakis, Nikos. *Zorba the Greek.* New York: Simon & Schuster, 1953.

Keyes Jr., Ken. *How to Enjoy Your Life in Spite of It All.* St. Mary, KY: Living Love Publications, 1980.

Kohn, Alfie. *No Contest: The Case Against Competition.* Boston: Houghton Mifflin, 1986.

Krishnamurti, J. *Freedom from the Known.* New York: Harper, 1969.

Kushner, Harold. *When All You've Ever Wanted Isn't Enough.* New York: Summit Books, 1986.

Levine, Stephen. *Meetings at the Edge: Dialogues with the Grieving and the Dying, the Healing and the Healed.* New York: Doubleday, 1984.

Lozoff, Bo. *We're All Doing Time.* Durham, NC: Human Kindness Foundation, 1985.

Mitchell, Jann. *Codependent for Sure: An Original Jokebook.* Kansas City, MO: Andrews and McMeel, 1992.

———. *Organized Serenity: How to Manage Your Time and Life in Recovery.* Deerfield Beach, FL: Health Communications, 1992.

Muller, Wayne. *Legacy of the Heart: The Spiritual Advantages of a Painful Childhood.* New York: Simon & Schuster, 1992.

Nouwen, Henri J. M. *Making All Things New: An Invitation to the Spiritual Life.* San Francisco: Harper, 1981.

Powell, John. *Happiness Is an Inside Job.* Allen, TX: Tabor Publishing, 1989.

Reynolds, David K. *A Thousand Waves: A Sensible Life Style for Sensitive People.* New York: William Morrow, 1990.

Roth, Robert. *Transcendental Meditation.* New York: Donald I. Fine, 1987.

Schachter-Shalomi, Zalman. *The Spiritual Elder: How to Enjoy the Harvest of a Lifetime.* Sounds True Recordings, 735 Walnut Street, Boulder, CO 80302. Audiotape.

Seven Taoist Masters: A Folk Novel of China. Translated by Eva Wong. Boston: Shambhala Press, 1990.

Sills, Judith. *Excess Baggage: Getting out of Your Own Way.* New York: Viking Press, 1993.

Steindl-Rast, Brother David. *The Grateful Heart*. Sounds True Recordings, 735 Walnut Street, Boulder, CO 80302, 1992. Audiotape.

Stevens, Barry. *Burst Out Laughing*. Berkeley: Celestial Arts, 1984.

———. *Don't Push the River: It Flows by Itself*. Moab, UT: Real People Press, 1970.

Sykes, Charles J. *A Nation of Victims: The Decay of the American Character*. New York: St. Martin's Press, 1992.

Trungpa, Chogyam. *Shambhala: The Sacred Path of the Warrior*. New York: Bantam Books, 1984.

Wilde, Stuart. *Miracles*. Taos, NM: White Dove International, 1983.

Williamson, Marianne. *Illuminata: Thoughts, Prayers, Rites of Passage*. New York: Random House, 1994.

Winokur, Jon. *Zen to Go*. New York: New American Library, 1989.

Wolinski, Kim. *Letting Go with All Your Might*. ReDecisions Institute, P.O. Box 6834, Denver, CO 80260, 1995.

By *Susan Jeffers, Ph.D.*

Books

Feel the Fear and Do It Anyway: Dynamic Techniques for Turning Fear, Indecision, and Anger into Power, Action, and Love*

Dare to Connect: Reaching Out in Romance, Friendship, and the Workplace**

Opening Our Hearts to Men: Learn to Let Go of Anger, Pain, and Loneliness and Create a Love That Works**

The Journey from Lost to Found: The Search That Begins with the End of a Relationship

End the Struggle and Dance with Life: How to Build Yourself Up When the World Gets You Down*

Thoughts of Power and Love

The "Fear-Less" Series (Affirmations)
Inner Talk for a Confident Day**
Inner Talk for a Love That Works**
Inner Talk for Peace of Mind**

Audio Workshops and Talks

A Fearbusting Workshop
The Art of Fearbusting
Flirting from the Heart
Opening Our Hearts to Each Other

Available (or can be ordered)
from your local bookstore.
Or call (1-800) 654-5126.

*Available in abridged and unabridged audiotape.
**Available in unabridged audiotape.